BLACK ATHLETE WHITE ATHLETE

Mental Strength: Winning The Battle That Others Don't See Now And In The Future

by
David Smith

B180 Basketball, Inc.
P.O. Box 2406
Midland, MI 48641-2406
www.b180basketball.com
Phone: 1-800-957-1275

© 2020 by David Smith. All rights reserved.

No part of this book may be reproduced, stored in a retrieval system, or transmitted by any means without the written permission of the author.

Published by B180 Basketball, Inc. 12-1-20

ISBN: (sc) 978-1-7325361-5-9
ISBN: (e) 978-1-7325361-4-2

Library of Congress Control Number: 2020921135

Any persons depicted in stock imagery are models, and such images are being used for illustrative purposes only.

Because of the dynamic nature of the Internet, any web addresses or links contained in this book may have changed since publication and may no longer be valid. The views expressed in this work are solely those of the author and do not necessarily reflect the views of the publisher, and the publisher hereby disclaims any responsibility for them.

Contents

Dedication..iv

Acknowledgments..v

Introduction..1

Five Challenges To Understand & Defeat To Gain Mental Strength...2

    Chapter 1: Injuries..39

    Chapter 2: Praying...48

    Chapter 3: Giving Your Best...56

    Chapter 4: Family Values..65

    Chapter 5: Advice From Others..75

    Chapter 6: Read, Read, Read..83

    Chapter 7: Learn and Make History..................................89

    Chapter 8: Give Back...97

    Chapter 9: Getting What You Want................................107

Bonus..108

Dedication

This book is dedicated to all of the athletes in the world. Your patience, determination, passion, and willpower to get through the difficult stages of your life is appreciated. You will do great things. This is my assist to you. Grow and give to others.

Acknowledgments

I would like to acknowledge and thank the Holy Spirit, Jesus Christ (Son of Man), God, and my parents, David C. Smith Sr. and Connie Smith. I'd also like to acknowledge the coaches that made a difference in my life, Mr. Jimmie Sanders, Mr. Steve Schmidt, Mr. Dean Lockwood, and Mr. Bob Taylor.

Finally, I'd like to acknowledge my elementary librarian, who made a difference, Mrs. Lynn Dent. Thank you.

Introduction

You may have mixed feelings right now. Many have felt that way. Take a moment to breathe. It will be all right. You've done the right thing by helping yourself and reading this book. Do the world and I a favor by continuing to read this book and many others. You will help trillions of people by doing so.

A lot has been going on in the past few years of your life. There has been a lot of changes in you, as well as the world around you. Take another breath. This will happen again and again, but you will become better prepared after reading this book.

What you can expect from this book is a solution to what is bothering you at a particular moment. As a person, athlete, student, and human being, you deserve the best because that's exactly what you have given up to this point in your life. This book will help uncover what you truly need to do to prepare yourself for the future and coming success.

Note: The views in this book are the author's views. For additional information on stress, anxiety, depression, or mental health, you can get information and resources from your health care provider.

Five Challenges To Understand & Defeat To Gain Mental Strength

- Feeling Important and Independent
- Peer Pressure & Suicide
- Dating & Relationships
- Family Disputes
- Stereotypes & Prejudices

Introduction

Feeling Important and Independent
Love

Love is something that everyone needs to receive, as well as give. Your life consists of immediate attention given to a select group of people on a daily basis. Your relationship with this group matters a lot, and it may consist of relatives or friends. Regardless of the make-up of the group, your heart vibes based on the individual relationships within the group. Some days, it will be good, and some days will be forgettable.

Learning to give unconditional love is the key to your own happiness. Give all of your love. That's what God is doing to you on a daily basis, so mimic the example given by God. Friends and relatives may hold grudges, push you to your boiling point, or disown you. Disregard their actions because a better day will be in the future for you, and their ways will eventually change. Most of them are viewing and analyzing you from your current status or by something that has recently happened. I know this is wrong. This is why you must follow God's will and ways. If you don't know much about the Kingdom of God, Jesus, or the Holy Spirit, I suggest you begin your journey now of seeking each of them. Upon completion, you should have a better understanding of the type of love that you should give.

Parents

Parents are important to many aspects of your life. An attempt must be made to establish and maintain a good relationship with both of them in order for you to maximize your full future potential. I say future potential because the groundwork is being established based on what you learn from your biological parents. There is no substitute. Give love to them and forgive, regardless if they are willing to give it back. There may be extreme instances that a good relationship with your parents is not possible. What you can always control is to give love and forgiveness as God does.

If one of your parents is not present in your life, seek them out and learn. It's vital for your complete development as a person in the world. If one parent is trying to stop you from seeking or knowing about the other parent, it may be because of their past relationship or experience with the other person. It's not about anything that you did. Continue to seek a relationship or bond with the parent that's missing in your life; it will uncover answers to questions you had in the past or still have.

Peers and Bullies

You never thought that it would happen to you. Someone is trying to make you look stupid in front of a crowd. This thought occurs in the minds of many individuals just like you around the world every day. The way you handle this, in some ways, determines your future.

There are three main ways that a person can respond to being bullied. One way is to accept the torture and situation as it unfolds by doing nothing, then walking away. The second way is to physically fight the person. This will solve nothing, so don't do this. The third way is to respond with unlimited kindness to the individual and situation. What I mean by kindness is that every response to the individual that is trying to bully you or anyone else is with kindness. Make a joke, smile, or turn the situation into something where everyone is happy, smiling, and no one is feeling hurt or down. This will be so tough to keep doing. If you are able to do this, it will prepare you to become a great leader in the future.

Although you respond with kindness, you still must tell someone about what is happening to you. Receiving peer pressure to do something that you don't want to do can be a horrible experience and leave an everlasting memory. When you put yourself in a position to only make a decision based on another individual's misguided thoughts, it makes you very vulnerable to experience a failure most of the time.

Between the ages of twelve and twenty-five, there will be numerous events that will involve you being pressured by others to do something that you do not want to do. The response you give is very important for your immediate future, as well as the long-term future.

What should you do? Well, you must trust your gut instinct and say "no" constantly. Most of the time, this will be the answer. Everything within you will be saying "no." It's the crowd of people that's making you feel like you are wrong, all because they want you to do what they want. Expect ridicule and harsh words when you make the decision to say "no" to peer pressure. Consider this their second wave of an attempt to make you do what they want, the crowd figures: "If we couldn't get him or her to say "yes" by cheering them on, we will make him or her feel worthless, then they will have to say yes."

The type of peer pressure will be different depending on your age between twelve and twenty-five. Even after the age of twenty-five, peer pressure exists and changes. The type of peer pressure could be being influenced to smoke cigarettes or an e-cigarette for the first time to taking drugs or having sex. Regardless of the situation, keep your faith, stand your ground firm by thinking of someone that is close to you, and your lifelong goal of making that person proud of you. Then say "no" and keep saying "no," no matter what.

Clicks and Groups

Deciding who to hang with daily is very important to your individual and social growth. The group of individuals that you choose to hang around with will basically represent who you are and where you want to be in life at the present moment and according to society. What I mean is that, if individuals that make up the group are thought of in a negative way by society, then society will consider you as a negative person that does the same things as the other members of the group. For example, if the friends that you hang out with currently are loud, disorderly, and don't take personal growth, education, or school seriously, then society (the people that see you on a daily basis with them as well as those people who you encounter) will think you are the same way, even if it's not true. The stigma of being a negative person or influence is sometimes hard to break.

So, what should you do if you are in a situation similar to this? The answer is that you must make a change to better yourself for the present and the future. That may be hard to do because you'll get resentment and negativity in words and actions from your former friends. You should handle the negativity the same way as if you were being bullied. In that particular situation, you are being bullied by your former friends. They will say things like, "Oh, you think that you are better than us. You're acting stuck up…." These are the things said in order to make you stay with the group.

The best type of people to be around or associate with are those that are great in some areas in life, personally or professionally, that you want to get better in, to learn from them.

They should be wise and gifted as leaders. The skills and ways of doing things that these individuals have should be seen being used positively. Society views these individuals in a positive way, as well. You will have to be very careful because in some cases, society may view a person in a positive way, but when they are not in public, they become negative and do bad things. If this happens, leave the individual or the group. Find new friends again. Be open to everyone and give them a chance. That's how you grow as a person. Overall, choose to hang around the individuals and groups of people that are going somewhere positive in life. Pay attention to their ways of doing the things that they do that make them great to hang around with.

Self-Identity

Who am I? This is a question a person must ask themselves constantly. You will come to find that there is a surface answer to this question, as well as a hidden one. You must understand how you were molded in order to know who you are and who you want to be. The task is to uncover clues to find out who you really are as an individual. Looking into your past in your family lineage helps you to uncover where you come from and how you were molded into the person you are today. This is only the surface. Understanding who you want to be and why you want to be that person are the hidden answers that you must find.

The world is full of individuals that can trace their family lineage back, almost to the beginning of time. Unfortunately, this is only half of what needs to be done. A true understanding of all of the individuals within your lineage will help you find out the answers to the difficult questions that you have. These are the questions that you may not have shared with anyone because you fear their reaction. Remember, the person in your lineage that you want to know more about was faced with the same question: *Who am I?* Analyze what they did and who they became as a person. You will then have a clear picture of what you must do to reach your own dreams and goals.

Commitment and Relationships

The feelings that you have for this person is unbelievable. Your own heart, soul, and body are in harmony. This is a vulnerable time for you because of this. Just because you have feelings, thoughts, and goals for the future of the relationship doesn't mean it will come true. Society and the person that you love; their thoughts, feelings, beliefs, and goals will meet you front and center. Sometimes, they may not want more than you want out of the relationship. Sometimes, they will want more than you do. Regardless, give love. This is what God wants. In return, you will grow, no matter what happens in the relationship. You'll have the opportunity to learn and grow as an individual for the person that you are really meant to be with.

Being committed to a relationship when your partner doesn't want to be will be so tough to do. Your emotions, thoughts, and feelings about them are strong and at the forefront. Remember to love yourself first. If you love yourself more than you love the person you are in a relationship with, it makes loving that person and handling rejections from them and society easier.

What I mean by loving yourself can be described in a variety of ways. To describe this, answer the following questions, "Do you exercise regularly? Do you eat healthily? Do you follow a personal and intellectual growth plan? And Do you care about your future and legacy?" The answers that you provide will let you know if you truly love yourself and are taking action to show it.

All in all, everyone will play the fool in love at least once. Learn from it. Love will take control of your thoughts, emotions, and actions. Believe in yourself, your goals, and your why. Give your absolute best in the relationship, pray, and let God do the rest. God uses relationships to mold you into the person that is needed for something great to come.

Being Alone

As you are lying down, thoughts may go through your mind about how you got to this point. Thoughts and feelings of sorrow and helplessness are at the forefront of your mind. This time alone can be of great value and benefit for you if you give it a chance. It may seem like nobody wants to be with or around you. This is not true. This time was put in place for you to grow and develop your gift.

I know this sounds strange, but you have a gift hidden inside of you, and this time is set aside for you to do something to bring it out. Whether it's listening to music, reading a book, writing, creating a video, praying, or talking to someone briefly, your gift will move forward on the days that you feel alone and by yourself. During these critical moments, you are carried by our father (God) with love. Don't give up because many individuals you are meant to help in the future are counting on you.

Social Media

Today, there are many ways to communicate with people. This is an advantage as well as a curse. Let's look at some of the advantages: 1) If you are in an emergency situation, you can simply use your social media presence to request help 2) Connecting with family and friends 3) Researching a job, career, or business. There are other advantages. These are just a few.

The disadvantages are: 1) Once you write something on your social media account, it's for the world to see, even if you didn't mean what you wrote 2) Prolonged use causes other areas of your life to suffer, such as losing sleep and not eating or exercising 3) Emotions are sometimes at its peak, and when something is written negatively, it has the potential to injure someone or cause them to take their own life.

When using social media, understand and give yourself a clear purpose for using the site you are on. Set time limits for its use in order to work on other areas of your life as well. This is very critical to your long-term health and well-being.

Taking Care of Siblings

Consider this situation, a parent or guardian is never at home or doesn't care. An older sibling may feel like they are the parent of their brother or sister. Whether it's cooking, cleaning, ironing, etc., the older sibling basically does it all to keep things a little stable. Even helping with homework. It may seem like there is no time to concentrate on their own self and the things they need. Resentment towards their parent or guardian is at a boiling point.

This situation is often played out across the United States as parents are working long hours and multiple jobs. The parent may have an alcohol, drug, or other addictive problem. The parent may also just be plain lazy. The pressure that is put on the older sibling can cause depression, anxiety, confusion, and feelings of helplessness. Before even reaching adulthood, overwhelming stress consumes them.

While it may seem like there is no way out of this situation, there is. As an individual and teen who is already going through changes, the older sibling must first concentrate on themselves. What I mean by this is in order to find out who you are, you must find out what truly makes you truly happy. I don't mean the typical immediate gratifications of physical pleasures, food, events, or people. The happiness that I'm referring to is the thing or things that you love to do even when you are feeling depressed, angry, or anxious. Despite the negative feelings, you have a burning desire to do it. This could be playing an instrument, singing, writing, drawing, building, gardening, poetry, etc. This is where most of your focus should be when times of caring for a sibling or a similar situation is controlling your daily life. Seek help from an honest and trusted adult or another individual. This may or may not have negative consequences for the parent or guardian. The underlying concern in the situation is you and your siblings. You must keep your happiness and positive personal growth as a priority in situations such as these.

Having a Job

Having a job can be a blessing, as well as a curse. Let's look at the positives of having a job during your teen and early adult years. First, you get to interact and learn from others while at work. The people you work with can make or break your long-term success. It depends on the type of job you have as well as the background and past experiences of the people you interact with. The type of jobs that improve your skills and prepare you for success as a person in the areas of self-discipline, promptness, spiritual growth, communication, speaking, leadership, sales, or creativity are the ones to seek.

At first glance, looking at these areas may make you feel scared or uneasy. However, improving in these areas will make your life easier and happier as you age. Learn at your own pace but do learn. The past experiences of your co-workers will be shared with you. Based on their views and how you interpret their stories, it will help mold you into the person you will be in the future. Another positive aspect of having a job is that you are learning that hard work is sometimes rewarded and sometimes not. You learn that it takes more than hard work to be a success. Based on your own past experiences, education, and continued pursuits, the actions you take outside of work, as well as what you learn from your co-workers will help decide whether you will develop your hidden gift or continue to be an employee. The negative of having a job is that the system (work/job) you chose to be trapped in may require you to work and perform duties in order to just stay employed to pay bills. In most cases, you have to work hard for long periods of time for low pay.

If working is not for you because you can't stand to be around people, then you stop yourself from being molded into a new person daily. Experiences, both good and bad, mold you. Working a job is not the only option. Starting your own business and including people that make you happy and stretch your personal and professional skills, as well as intellect, will increase your overall growth, no matter if the business is a success or not. You will find that the business that you start will give you a feeling of power that you've never felt before. Embrace it and grow as a person inside and out.

Introduction

Peer Pressure and Suicide
Thoughts

The hidden secret that controls your life is inside of you. To have the power to choose your own destiny is a want from every individual. If they only took the time to understand what is happening to them on a daily basis, they would find that they are controlled by their thoughts.

Along with emotions, a person's thoughts make them who they are. Let's take, for example, a person breaks up with their long-time girlfriend or boyfriend. They may experience feelings and emotions of heartbreak, guilt, suicide, and loss. Their friends may add on to it by asking the wrong questions or leaving nasty comments. The person's every thought would be ultimately directed towards negativity. In turn, the outcomes they would experience daily would be negative, as well. This is a hidden secret that many have written and spoken about, and only a few people really understand.

In order to change your present and future situations, you must first learn to control your thoughts. Turn a negative thought into a positive as quickly as you can. In some instances, it may feel like your mind is being bombarded with nothing but negative thoughts. In this case, you must deny the thoughts and stay speaking, thinking, and writing positive things about the same thing you were thinking negatively about. This process takes time to develop. Learn to get a true understanding of who you are as a person and where you want to go. Read and pray as much as you can daily. Eventually, you will gain control of your thoughts as well as your life. Emotions influences thoughts, so control your emotions. Make both your thoughts and emotions good.

Family History

Sometimes, the feelings of loneliness and emotions of hurt won't leave you alone. They return over and over in your heart, being both low and high. Just because a family member's life was stressful and filled with negativity and loss doesn't mean that you inherited their problems. It's a choice that you have to make, whether to accept their situation and live through their pain or choose your own path that you create based on your thoughts, emotions, dreams, and goals.

The challenge that a person faces when dealing with family members' problems is that you feel that it's your problem because they are family, and they need you or can only talk to you at that point and time. The family member may resort to using drugs, alcohol, or other negative suppressants to help alleviate the pain they feel. You see this firsthand and may think to yourself, "This must be the best way to cope with problems." In reality, it's not.

Your family history should be defined by each member's unique ability to add positive value to the world. This means rejecting negative family coping strategies and developing a plan to handle stress in a way that adds good value to long-term goals.

Feeling Down

The moments of feeling down and of nobody caring will be plentiful. During these moments and stages, much praying and finding of yourself (self-awareness/development) must be pursued. Answering the questions *Who am I? and Why am I here?* is important during the process. Develop a clear picture of who you really are as an individual here on earth at this particular time period. Looking at your past and then coming to a quick conclusion about your past actions during an event will not be enough. Don't look to the past. It has happened already. If you continue to look back on the past, it will eventually cause illness and death. You have to dig deeper. Think spiritually, emotionally, and ethically. Where do you see yourself as it relates to life? What do you believe will happen when you eventually die? Do you believe in God? Do you believe in God's Kingdom? If you don't believe in either, ask yourself, "Have I really done my part in trying to build a relationship with God?" Answering these questions will help you believe in Jesus, the Holy Spirit, God, and God's Kingdom. You won't just make a decision because of all the bad things that have happened or are happening to you.

Feeling down can cause unwanted stress and anxiety. Nobody likes feeling sad, unwanted, alone, and worthless. It hits to the core of your inner self hard like a brick hitting a car's windshield. Like a car, you have to be repaired, and you can't do it alone all of the time. You'll have to find someone or others that relate best to what you are going through. Once you find the right person, be completely honest and open when talking to them. This will be the only way to completely recover from feeling down.

Long-Term Goals

Don't do it for your parents. Don't go on for the person that you are in a relationship with. Don't go on for someone who has mentored or helped you. Make the decision to defeat peer pressure and feelings of suicide by moving forward in a positive way because you are doing it for you and you only. Knowing that the time period that you are currently in will pass and things, people, and situations will pass by just as time passes. The vision of yourself in one year, two years, five years, or twenty years will be different than what it is now. Consider yourself building you for the future. The bad things must happen in order to build the right you for the future. You were perfectly designed and equipped to withstand what you are going through at this particular moment. Once you weather the storm, you become battle-tested, and it shows that you are a winner and the only one that can create who you will become.

When going through your daily interactions, start it by mentally preparing. That means creating a morning routine that will prepare you mentally, spiritually, and physically to help build the future you.

Getting Help

I know you think that no one will understand what you've been through or are currently going through. In a way, you are right. Nobody can be you and experience how you feel about things. What they can do is put themselves wholeheartedly into your situation to feel and interpret your experience and feelings. The interpretation they receive will be as accurate as what you honestly and clearly open up and tell the individual. In order to be who you truly were meant to be, you must let go and get help. Know that God planned this exact moment that you decided to seek help. Yes, it will be the right person who you are talking to about it. Peer pressure and feelings of suicide are very challenging and can change your future in an instance. This is why it's very important that you tell someone if you are being pressured to do something that you are not fully committed to doing. The decision you make will show that your beauty did shine through. The results will show.

Impressing Others

It's not worth making others feel happy if your gut feeling and intuition are telling you something different. Go with your gut feeling. The mind, body, and universe have a way of working together that brings forth energy. This energy, as I will call it, sends messages that are connected to your thoughts, feelings, and body. If you ignore it and decide to please the crowd or friends, guilty thoughts tend to follow because deep down, there's a feeling that you may have made the wrong decision.

Impressing others can lead a person to lose or damage relationships with close friends and relatives. In the end, the group or individual that you are trying to impress will hold the event against you as a type of mockery in the future. So, it's best to clearly think about what you are about to do before doing it. Believe in yourself and love yourself first.

Friends

Your friends and family should save you. Pay attention to what they are saying, then filter out the negative advice from what is positive. Analyze it against immediate as well as long-term goals and dreams. Does it fit? If it does, then you must make the correct decision. Understand that many individuals may have traveled a similar path that you have chosen. It's now up to you to make a decision to go against the normal path in order to create a new reality. This will make you unique. Discover the hidden message that was given to you. It's a must. This will cause a dramatic shift in your situation based on your belief and commitment to doing what is right and just.

Friends may go overboard and say things that make you feel uneasy. This is a test that will determine where you will go in life based on your current decisions. You must analyze the situation and truly trust what is just. A friend is someone who understands who you are and also believes in you. It doesn't matter if they are in your life daily or not. What matters most is their belief and understanding, support, and acceptance of you. Deciding whether to make new friends or not will always be a challenge. In order to grow, you must understand and be clear about what you want out of life. Then create situations and events that make you meet new people.

Bullies

When it's all said and done, the battle will not be between a bully or an individual that is trying to make you do something that you don't want to do. The battle will be with your own inner self. How do you see yourself at this exact moment? Why do you see yourself that way? Where did the current vision of yourself come from? Who do you blame for how you currently see yourself? The answers that you provide to these questions will help you discover the root cause of the inner battles that you have with yourself.

It may show that you have been bullying yourself into believing and accepting certain people, things, and events. In order to overcome the outside pressure or influences from another individual, you must stop bullying yourself with self-doubt, non-belief, and criticism. Instead, feed your inner self with praise, love, support, and, most of all, the faith that you can overcome any and all situations, events, circumstances, relationships, and people by seeking truth in what is unknown to you at the present moment.

The difficult period that you are currently in will eventually pass, and a better time will come. All your deepest wishes and dreams will begin to come true during this time.

It starts with you changing your inner thoughts about yourself.

Overcoming a situation with a bully takes courage and support from others. As you seek support by telling someone about the situation, begin to look inside yourself because the long-term answer is found inside of you.

Saying No

Never deny the truth when faced with uncertainty. You must be aware of who you really are. This means understanding what has caused you to be in the current situation that you are in and the belief that you have about what is happening or about to happen. The person, group, or thoughts trying to persuade you or force you to do something is doing so because you are letting it happen in the first place. Think carefully as you decide on what to do next. Know that whatever decision you make is or was the right one and that you gave your best. If you can believe this and trust that what you gave was your absolute best in that particular moment, then you set yourself free from guilt, regret, and sorrow. You are able to grow from the situation and change into the person that you truly want to become.

Keep in mind that you are not doing anything or making a decision for anyone but the best interest in its entirety for yourself. Ultimately, over the course of your life, you will come to understand that the decision you made in a particular event was needed in order for you to experience certain events, meet individuals, and fail in order to become the person that you are today.

Why it Matters

The hurt, let-downs, guilt, sorrow, and other negative emotions that you may feel are caused by you and you alone. You have the power to change anything that you are currently going through if and only if you are able to change who you believe you are. You must see yourself as a piece or pieces of a puzzle sent to make the world better. The puzzle will not be complete until you know what you were meant to give to the world solely out of true love and acceptance of who you are.

Peer pressure and thoughts of suicide will constantly try to force you to make a quick decision based on unclear and sometimes false illusions about a situation. Your past experiences have prepared you to make the decision that you must make. Controlling your emotions and excluding the negative emotions and consequences based on your decision will help guide you to the truth.

Dating & Relationships
Living Together

Initially, what you perceive is right won't be. When you decide to live with the person you are in a relationship with, everything changes. It's now "We," not "I" or "Me." Decisions, values, beliefs, and daily routines must be discussed and agreed upon. This may involve discussing your living arrangement as well as your future plans with a third party (counselor, etc.).

A complete understanding and acceptance of your significant other's race, culture, heritage, values, past, and traditions must be made. It's a must. You then must share yours and ask for understanding and acceptance on your behalf. Once this is done, you are able to move to the next step in the journey. This involves coming into a specific agreement on what cultures, heritages, values, beliefs, spirituality, and traditions you plan to adopt as a couple. You are beginning your journey to becoming one. Once this is done, you will have conquered more than some married couples. Again, it's a journey, so ongoing discussions, going to family gatherings on both family sides, and counseling can be done to assist you with the process. Living with someone is a huge leap. It's very different from living by yourself. It's a commitment to share. The sharing and other commitments that you both agree to will either help solidify the relationship you are in or prepare you for the next one. If either person is not totally committed to the daily tasks of what it takes to live together, then this will be a sign that your relationship needs help. The outcome of your current relationship will be solely up to the actions that each individual takes to improve the relationship and make it one.

The Big Picture

When two become one, that's when God is happy. If you don't believe in God, then either, 1) this book is not for you 2) You believe in something else 3) You need to find who you truly are and what you were born to do. Does this mean that every relationship is the same? The answer to this is no. You must seek and find your true self before you find the answer to salvation. The journey to find who you really are will take a commitment and rebirth to what you currently believe about who you are. When you are filled with hurt, what you do in that particular moment sometimes identifies as well as traps your hidden gifts. To help you on your journey to find and commit to someone else in a relationship, you must know what you were born to do. Then you must develop the gift given to you and give it to the world. Finding what you have hidden inside of you requires a cleansing of your soul and an analysis of where you currently are at as an individual and where you want to be in the future.

Oneness

Money will not make your significant other believe in what you were called to do. This is a dilemma that continuous prayer, belief, and understanding will either strengthen your relationship or break it apart. To become one, you must know and be confident in your gift. Then, wholeheartedly accept what answer is given to you by God first; and then by the world.

Based on your choice to accept or reject who you are and what you were born to give to the world, life will bless you. Marijuana, alcohol, or any other drug is not the answer to your problems. It makes the current situation that you are in worse. You might say some of the things are from the earth, so it's good for you. Well, there are plants grown that come from the earth, and if you take a few bites of it, you will die.

To become one in your relationship, trust in every facet must be given to your partner. Growth comes in times of despair and unrest. There will be times when the thoughts of leaving seem easier than going through what you are about to go through. God delivers on all of his promises, and if your love for the person is true, the decision that is made by God will always be the right one.

Friends versus Relationship

Having a friend is a choice. Choosing a friend over the person you are in a personal relationship with is a decision you will have to live with. Friends try to compete for your love, trust, time, and companionship just as much as the person you love the most and are in a relationship with. Your happiness and personal growth come from being around both your friends and your partner. Being around both helps to develop you into a new individual. Love changes it all and can save you from pain. How is this, you may ask. When the heart loves, it gives it all. There is no half-loving someone. So, you must be careful and use your wit to uncover your true friends. This will help you from losing someone that could have been in your life forever. Your best friend will be with you when you are not you. Knowing what to do in order to help you is not a choice with this individual. They understand everything that is going on and still believe in you. The choice now is to either keep your best friend or the person that you are in a relationship with. They both know almost everything about you, and for the most part, they both care about your well-being. The only difference is the physical interaction with your partner. Choose them over your best friend only if you can picture and truly see yourself growing old and happy with him or her. That person must have the same vision too. You will find that your best friend will still be there in the end.

Cheating

Lives can be ruined because of cheating that goes on in a personal relationship. Jail, death, hurt, pain, and deceit reign superior if cheating is continuously present in a relationship. If you truly love someone and care for them, then let them do as they want. You will find that if a person truly wants to be with you and only you, they will not want anyone else. They may make mistakes because no person is free of sin or mistakes. The cheater realizes what they did and what they are about to lose. The person that was cheated on realizes what they committed to in the relationship and what they are about to lose. The growth comes from belief in God and the person that you truly love finding God. It's God's will for you to be together if you stay together. All answers lie with belief in what you both created that was good in the relationship. If there is no belief in what God has in store for both of you, then it's time to move on and use the relationship as a lesson. You will be a better person because of this situation. You must trust the molding of yourself that is currently taking place in your life and pray daily.

Overprotection from either person involved will cause the other person in the relationship to leave. Clearly understand and envision what you want in the future. I'm talking 10 to 30 years from now. If you can truly envision yourself growing old with the person that you are with, then cheating on them is always a gamble, and nothing that you do or say will count to make cheating seem right in the heat of the moment. If you do cheat, the only thing you will depend on is trust and belief in what you've done for the relationship and will do in the future. It's better to just grow together and discover life as one united by God. Don't hurt the ones that you love most.

Hurt

Nothing will compare to the pain that you feel throughout your body when you are hurt by the one you are in love with. Minutes seem like days. Hours pass by like years. So much has happened to you, the relationship, and the person that you are dating. The beauty in them is real, but neither you nor them sees it. The fate of your pain is in God's hands, and you must believe that the best outcome will reveal itself because of this fate. I'm not saying that things will turn out bad. What I'm saying is that if you've truly given everything; are still trying to give, and you are hurting, this may be a sign from above telling you to let the pain that you feel guide you to serenity. How is this done, you may ask. Knowing that there is a true love felt by you, and either you or the person that you are in a relationship with doesn't agree with it. The presence of God is guided by the person with the genuine love. When they hurt, they feel how God feels when He is rejected. The hurt is powerful and unmatched. The feeling puts you in a position to begin a relationship with God. Ask for continued guidance through the pain that you are feeling.

Letting Go

There will never be a perfect moment or situation to leave or let go of a feeling that you have for someone. Your whole soul was involved, so the pain you feel is real, and the recovery time will be needed to create a new you. Never imagining that this time would come, it's here and now. You have to pick up the pieces because it's in the plan that God truly has for you. Undeniable trust in God must be had. Letting go or being let go from a person, place, situation (even death), or event requires you to understand and be truthful about everything for yourself and to yourself. When you are truthful, you will understand why the current event is happening and what you need to do to become a more complete person. True love given by anyone to someone else takes patience and commitment. The feelings and emotions in this process reflect the pain that the love given has experienced. Letting go is a process of understanding the past and present, then using it to prepare yourself for a better future.

Finding You

To be given it all and let it go without thinking is a common fault. Many spend their adult years filled with guilt, regret, and hurt because of this. Never let a past event dictate a negative quick action or response. To get over what you are currently going through, true consciousness of who you are and what you were born to do must be established and practiced. The world will give easy passes to what seems like glory. If it wasn't what you were truly meant to give to the world, then sorrow and unrest will persist.

A hundred-dollar bill is unable to talk and share its true gift because it failed to improve itself daily, and therefore, the majority of the time, it will decrease in value first. The only reason it has value is because of what it's perceived to be. Underneath, the hundred-dollar bill hurts and yearns for the truth. Learn to love and forgive. This will open the door to the Kingdom of God, and you will be able to find the true you.

Hidden beneath the glamour and glow of external mirages is a place that seems non-existent to many individuals. The inner self can't be discovered by the ordinary eye or happenings around you. This place is sacred and can only be found and understood through prayer, belief, and seeking. When you decide to find the real you, that is, the person you were born to be; the gifts that you have been blessed with from God will be discovered. These gifts help to define you but do not complete you. Your gifts, oneness with God, and the giving of yourself and your gifts to the rest of God's children will make you fully complete.

Daily distractions, negative thoughts, and external temptations can be defeated with positive thoughts, positive words, meditation, meaningful prayers, positive visions, and positive deeds as a complete person. Finding yourself then can take a lot of falling down (failing) and having the strength and determination to get back up. By getting back up, you are able to learn from your failures as well as gain inner peace, strength, and confidence from the experience. To truly find oneself, a person must ignore what's seen by the naked eye and turn to what's within. That is the true, pure, Godly thoughts. If this is done, they will then begin the journey to becoming free.

Communication

"You don't understand me" are the words that you may be thinking towards your significant other. All the pain, rejection, anger, and guilt from the previous years of your life are at the forefront. What can the other person that you love do or say to make you become more at peace? You may be wondering. Well, there is nothing that can be done until you willingly begin to open your heart, mind, and actions towards yourself. Understanding yourself, your strengths, and weaknesses within the relationship, as well as being a person of value, will begin the process of developing a positive communication channel with the person you are currently in a relationship with. Communication is the backbone of a relationship. If you are able to understand the other person and their beliefs, customs, and ways of living, harmony can exist. If you are able to mentally put yourself in their position before you speak and acknowledge your own true faults, then the relationship can be nourished. Communication in a relationship, whether the relationship is intimate, physical, or just friendly, is the key to expanding the glory of your intended purpose in life. Be open but careful. Remember your past faults and failures. Talk with a purpose. These things are needed when communication in a relationship needs to be established, improved, or nourished.

Forgiveness

Seek forgiveness from the Kingdom of God. As you prepare for life after a rough relationship, begin to prepare yourself for undeniable hurt, pain, and sorrow. Despite the feelings that you will endure, forgiveness of the other person in your relationship must be done. You have to forgive others in order to be forgiven for any and all wrongs that you have done or will do. Pour out your heart to what you believe is right by God. If you are able to forgive the person even though you know what they did to you was done on purpose, then your access to a better life will begin to take form.

Cheating, lying, abuse, and jealousy reign supreme in relationships that will ultimately end in someone being scorned. When this happens, the world is at the mercy of the scorned individual. Every thought, emotion, and feeling that the scorned individual has is of revenge and regret. To defeat this powerful rage expressed inside and out, the other person's pure and absolute forgiveness must be given inside of the scorned person's heart.

How is this done? Prayers without feelings or thoughts of hate, revenge, pity, sorrow, or deceit will effectively open access to God. The next step is to forgive the person who hurt you without remorse, revenge, or regret. Instead, think, pray, and bless the individual. Continue to love and praise the person in a positive manner. After being hurt, if you are able to love the person the same way you did at the beginning of the relationship, no one can hurt you or make you have feelings of pain or regret. You succeed because you are able to forgive.

Family Disputes
Money

Never again will you cry for money because of a family member. Money causes pain, hurt, deceit, envy, death, and more. It also causes happiness, belief, joy, and excitement. Why? Well, to reach a certain level by society's view, a person needs money. If you can denounce money and instead fall in love with the gift that was blessed to you at birth, then money will follow. Too many lives have been ruined and hurt because of money. Whether it was because of too much or too little money, the outcome remained the same. Let go of life's initial view and look deeper into what money can do if controlled for doing good for the world. Family disputes damage an individual because of the lack of control over money. You may be wondering, how do you control money? The answer is making it work for you. Learn how money works.

Generation after generation, your family has worked or given their time for money in some capacity. When pain, sorrow, lack, hurt, and envy are present when it involves money, you must stay grounded in your belief and in your ultimate dream. Follow the original course that you designed. Arguments, loss, and failure may occur. This is God's stepping stone for you to mend a family's fortune. Don't let money be the cause of a detachment from your family. Endure the emotional journey and learn to make money work for you. Stay in control.

Independence

What you are going through right now will pass by. The arguments that you had with your family member is because they or you did not want to let go of the way things used to be. Acceptance of the way things are going currently is a challenge to both of you. Growth and maturity have happened to you as well as your family member. Not truly wanting to let go of the joy and bliss of years past and the safety for all are present. When people truly grow, a new understanding of their uniqueness and the divine nature and growth within has to happen. In your dispute with your family member, love exists, but it is blinded by fear and anxiety of what's to be expected from the person you've become and everyone else involved in the dispute. To be independent requires maturity, an understanding of what is true, serenity, and love of all of God's creations. The learning process to be independent requires different sacrifices and challenges for everyone. When you decide to stand up for your independence, you begin the process and journey to finding God. Most people never find truth or God because of worldly vices and temptations that are presented to them. The protection and security that your family member is trying to eagerly defend are normally their own thoughts for your divine path to truth and discovery of God. Understand that love will always exist from your family member, and there will be better days. As time passes, an understanding of what was done to you, what you did, as well as what you must do next will occur. Acceptance and action will be a choice that each person must make.

Discipline

It's time to get back up again. I know it hurts. I know there's pain. You've been through so much, and it still seems like no one understands or cares. You may ask yourself, "How can this be when I've given everything that I've got?" The countless times that you've fallen down is disciplining you to see glory. Every hurt, thought, wish, and regret builds you up to become a new person. That is if you choose to get up. Coming this far and now turning around is not a choice. Look forward, seeing the new you do exactly what you dreamed to be doing. Without discipling your actions and mind to do and think positive, being strong, and forgetting all things negative, self-pity will reign.

How do you discipline your actions and mind? Well, change everything that is negative that you are currently doing and begin by spending the mornings with God. Whether 10, 20, or 60 minutes, discipline yourself to start your mornings in unselfish thought, gratitude, forgiveness, and peace. It's up to you to find the light. Remember what you've been through and forgive everything about it. If you can do this, then say hello to a new disciplined you!

Give love freely to everyone, and you begin to be more complete. The world, as well as family members, will sometimes give unwanted negativity towards you because of who they think you are. They have not lived your life and been through what you have. So, think and believe that their negativity as not being real. It's an emotional phase that they are going through just as you are at the moment. Your family member or friend is unable to accept and relate to their true inner self within that gives love and is Godly as the situation exists. Daily discipline to the simple things, such as showing gratitude and love for just being in existence as well as taking time for meditation, will help to discipline the actions of the mind towards serenity.

Without A Parent

"What do I do now?" is a question that you ask yourself. Whether your parents played a part in your life and were there for you or if you've never met or seen them, this is a question that runs through the mind over and over again. It must be answered, but how can you begin to answer this question if pity, hurt, negativity, resentment, and regret exists? Never before have you felt so strongly about two individuals. The heart yearns for truth. In order to find who you are, the love and forgiveness of your parents are the starting point. Picture God forgiving you and continuing to love you when you do things that are not in correlation with who you were born to be. This is only a glimpse of what was experienced by the two individuals that shared in bringing you into the world.

Loneliness, anxiety, and hurt may be present currently. This is because of your lack of forgiveness. Never underestimate the power of forgiveness. Forgive them completely without remorse. Give your all in every facet to make your life and love for what's to come in your life complete. Nothing will ever compare to a day fishing with your biological dad or a conversation over a cup of tea with your biological mother. Make it happen for a better tomorrow for you. The peace that it will bring will unlock prayers to a new way of life.

Arguments and Talking Back

Please calm down and think about what you said or will say. You may have just gone through something that you never thought would happen. Understand that your life will change for the better because of this. That's if you truly believe in what you are arguing for, and you still care for and love the person that you are arguing with, regardless of the outcome. You may be hurting and feel that there is no way out right now. Use the entire situation as a stepping stone. A kind of aha moment to discover who you are and what you are supposed to live and do in the world. Your emotions may be at a high level. Harness the thoughts of anger and instead think of things that make you smile. The pain, negative thoughts, and guilt will be defeated after an argument with someone if you are willing to truly forgive them. Take the time to truly examine what it is that you are arguing about. Ask yourself, is it really worth what you said or currently feel about the person? Forgive them, regardless. Love them endlessly and never stop. This is a must to be able to overcome your current situation and reach your future dreams.

It's going to take some time to truly understand your full obligation to what your gift is to the world. It's possible to never discover your gift if your thoughts and actions are continuously negative. It's hard to grow as a person and for your gift to be nurtured in negativity. Love hurts, and at the same time, there's a feeling of joy, bliss, and excitement. Learn to control your heart to love endlessly, regardless of the current situation. This gives you power and control over your life and the situation.

Ignoring Someone and Holding Grudges

It's impossible to ease the pain you feel if you ignore the person or people you are angry with. Your thoughts stay on them and why you are mad at them. It only makes you think of this group or individual more. It also makes you think negatively. Therefore, most things and life events that are experienced will seem to be negative to you as well. In order for you to get over your pain and begin to experience stress-free happiness, then learn to not ignore or hold grudges. Forgive the person or people that you are mad at and love them.

Actually, speak the words "I love and forgive _____." This will open the doors to freedom and a new state of consciousness for you. This will not be easy to do, but relax, keep trying, and the better you get at this, the more changes for the good in your life will there be.

Regardless of the circumstances of what's been done to you, forgive and commit to giving love. Many people go through life holding grudges and being resentful. This wears them down and causes stress, pain, and, eventually, poor health as they age. You are at a crossroads in your life. Make the best decision by being a source of unconditional love.

Introduction

Reuniting & Building a Lasting Bond

In the end, you were born to be happy and successful through all of life's situations and trials. That's why you are able to stand after a failure or let-down. When I say stand, I mean think, do, or say something positive that strengthens you or someone else.

Think of the heartbreaks that you've experienced. You are still here. You've gotten back up time and time again. When thoughts raced through your mind telling you to just give up and let everything go, you didn't listen. You are reading this book, so something great is being nurtured within you. For not giving up, you've won a very important battle. You are a winner!

Whether you are reuniting with a loved one, friend, or a significant other, the love that you shared for each other begins to shine and show every time you are around that person. Tell them how happy that you are to be back in their life. It doesn't make a difference whether they tell you first or not. Give love and begin to live happier because you have chosen to reunite with someone that means a lot to you.

In order to build a strong and lasting bond with a family member that you truly love, you must stay in contact with them in some way. Whether you talk on the phone or visit them weekly, keep the relationship strong through contact. A simple phone call saying, "Hello, I just wanted to hear your voice and tell you that I love you," makes all the difference. Remember, time and the years will begin to seem to go by fast to you. A loved one will eventually die. Make the most of the relationship now by doing things with them as if they didn't have much time left on earth to live. A lasting bond is something that even death will not be able to take away from you because you will know and feel the love of the person even after they are gone.

Stereotypes & Prejudices
They Say I'm Different

Your difference gives you unmatched power in this world. The problem that must be solved is how to use the differences that others see in you in a good way. It should benefit you as well as the world. The difference could be, for example, a physical disability or a perception of a person being very quiet and not wanting to make friends. Society may also view race, religion, gender, or uncommon views of the world as being different. This is due to the lack of a true understanding of the person that is labeled different.

People in society have not experienced what you've experienced up to this point in your life. They may tend to view others through their own outlook of the world and the current situation that is presently upon the both of you. Fighting, cursing and showing hate for the person in society only makes things worse. Choose to be grounded in your own beliefs and views. Respect and understand their beliefs and views. Doing this gives you the power to withstand the negativity that will be shown towards you. Think clearly about what and who you are perceived to be by the people in society. If it's not the right view, then you will have to decide if the situation that you are in is really worth explaining to the individuals involved who you really are. If it's not worth it, then simply forgive them and learn how to better communicate with those that negatively view you. I know forgiving the person is going to be tough to do, but understand that by doing this, you begin to mold yourself into the person that you are wishing and really want to be.

Having a Disability

Take a second to look back at what you've been through. It may be tough to see how much pain you've been able to handle. Though you are wishing that things were different, you've been blessed with something that nobody else has or will ever have. This exact moment, your exact struggle, and your belief of becoming the best that you can be, have all happened for a reason. Your gift to the world is hidden within your suffering. Having the courage to go through the difficulty of accepting and acknowledging a disability brings you closer to consciousness.

Be peaceful in your acceptance of what is true. Understand why. Believe that this journey that you are on will conclude with happiness, serenity, and accomplishments if and only if you do not use your disability as a reason for your failure in any form. Rise above mediocracy, blame, guilt, sorrow, and hate by using your disability as a reason to bring your gift to the world. There will be others with similar disabilities in years to come, and they are waiting, wanting, and praying for you to do what you are supposed to do. Make it happen. Believe in the Kingdom of God. You will leave a permanent footprint.

Culture Clash

Whether a person is of African descent, European descent, Asian descent, or any other ethnicity, the same ferocious and negative type of person can exist in them. The person could be calm and happy on the outside, but deep down, anger and hatred runs deep because of how things are in life. How can this be? What that particular person has been through, as well as their ways of interpreting every past and present event, have caused them to be exactly who they are today. Looking at this from another view, if the person is on the surface negative, aloof, and mean, they may, deep down, be kindhearted and peaceful. The defining factor is what has happened to this person in his or her lifetime and how they have interpreted each event.

Race, gender, and cultural ways of doing things have divided many households and nations. It has killed many people. When you can truly understand that it's not the outside person you should judge, but the person inside, you will be able to find true peace and happiness in your own life. Faith, hope, love, and forgiveness will not be the answer unless a person does these things as God does. That means to give unconditional love to all.

Rich and Poor

You cannot take it with you. Give it freely and find truth. Why worry about money then? Yes, it's important, but the ultimate challenge is to find out what you can do better than anyone else in this world to earn what you feel and believe you deserve. Many judgments are made by individuals who have a lot of money and those that have none. They both may view the opposing social class as spoiled, unworthy, or handfed. Look past your upbringing and ways of living and find out what value you can bring out of you to offer to the world. It truly hurts when a person that you know is qualified for a position but is not given the opportunity because of their upbringing and way of life about money. Their background is perceived negatively, so they are overlooked.

In response to this, give back and give love. Show love. Forgive whatever experience that you have been through and make an honest decision. If you are seeking a job, hiring an individual, or seeking a business opportunity, disarm your pre-judgments and innate prejudices. Instead, immerse in the meeting and put yourself in the shoes of the person that you are meeting with and truly feel how you would about yourself if you were initially created under the same circumstances. Then prepare yourself to make a decision accordingly and regardless of their race or socioeconomic background.

Whether a person is rich or poor, they may have the same underlying problems in their lives. Money just covers up what is normally visible in the less fortunate. Believe in yourself. Know that what you are currently experiencing is something that you must go through to get your reward. A person who has riches that are blessed by God's will has the ultimate success. They also have the command to give love as God gives to all of his children.

Gender and its Meaning

Who are you? The answer to this question alone sets you free. Know that religion, society, relatives, and friends don't matter in your decision. What matters is the view, the innate long-term view that you have for yourself. Close your eyes and imagine yourself twenty years from now. Imagine who you are mentoring. Do you have children? Do you have grandchildren? How do you want to make their lives better? Is it only all about you? If it is, then this lifetime will go by fast, and what you think was an accomplishment really won't be. Take time to find out who you really are. Find out your true likes and dislikes by experiencing it firsthand. Think about how you were raised. Then and only then are you able to know who you are, and you'll believe it. Right now, you may not believe it. Become a truth-finding individual. Find a strength that you can depend on and use this strength to help others. In turn, your strengths will help you find out who you are.

Chapter 1

Injuries

Why Me?

Never thinking that this day would come, a lot of questions begin to enter the mind. Pain, regret, denial, and shock of what has happened to you dominate your emotions. The questions of "What am I supposed to do next?" and "Why me?" are key questions that will constantly be in your thoughts. Whether the injury is serious (career-ending) or not, a feeling of invincibility exists in every athlete. Never truly paying attention to what other athletes have gone through as it relates to injuries that they may have had in the past has hindered initial progress for your own growth and recovery.

Injuries can mold a person into who they were truly meant to be, or it can cause depression and destroy a dream. See clearly what actions you are taking, and if they are negative, find any and all help possible to turn your actions and thoughts positive. Get the people that decide to help you to also assist with answering the question, "Why Me?" This question will continuously come to mind. Similar to the way that you thought about the sport that you love. When the question "Why Me?" enters your thoughts, you must be able to answer it positively and challenge yourself to take on the next chapter of your life with determination and the seeking, curiosity, and heart of a child.

Different Types of Injuries

There are various types of injuries. Injuries could be physical, mental, spiritual, or emotional. The way that you respond to an injury determines the person you will become. Although the injury may have become a major setback, the thoughts that enter the mind can cause further damage. Pain, anger, and regret are like asbestos and mold growing in your favorite gym. Too much asbestos and mold could destroy the gym permanently. Regain a positive attitude, positive thoughts, faith, courage, and love for yourself. Not anyone else. Just you. Love yourself for once wholeheartedly. Learn to understand who you are currently and who you need to become in order to make yourself happy in this lifetime. What follows are descriptions of each type of injury that could occur. They are physical injury, mental injury, spiritual injury, or emotional injury.

Physical Injury

These injuries can occur during physical activity or daily happenings. They can be minor, such as a scrape or bruise on the body. They also can be major, such as a break or tear of a body part. The way that a person rehabs and thinks after the occurrence of the injury dictates the majority of the initial success that they will have when recovering. Physical injuries can also occur when a person is consumed by only physical gratifications that are in the world.

Mental Injury

This type of injury occurs when a person's mind is neglected, used, manipulated, or denied. When a person is guided down a path, let's say playing a sport, for instance, they are putting a lot of time and effort into developing their skills and body for the sport. If the athlete, relatives, coaches, trainers, or organization fails to provide equivalent time, resources, and support to develop and train the mind, a mental injury occurs. The athlete fully develops their physical skills and body for the particular sport, but their mind is injured. Most individuals are in disbelief and a state of frustration.

In order to overcome a mental injury, acceptance of reality is the first step. Then, acknowledging that the mental injury exists and must be improved is next. After the acknowledgment, self-searching, and answering the questions "Who am I?" and "Who do I want to be?" has to be completed. Examples of a mental injury are not being able to read, write, or speak fluently. It can also be the inability to cope with various worldly happenings and emotional states.

Spiritual Injury

A spiritual injury occurs when a person neglects to truly attempt to find meaning and faith. It can occur when a person follows a meaning, religion, faith, or spirituality and is not truly committed to it. It can also occur when a person chooses not to follow anything at all. By not following or seeking anything, it could be both good and bad. It's a state when hope and hopelessness run through the mind of the person. If they can look deep into their ways (hidden and unhidden) and learn to understand why they think the way that they do, they will be able to accept who they are at that particular moment and find spirituality.

Emotional Injury

Emotional injuries occur when in the present moment a person handles a situation in a negative way or in a way that is unusual to their character. The events leading up to the current situation may be the underlying cause, but it's not recognized by the individual. A negative emotion hurts not only the individual but the entire world. It's important to understand how you respond to things that you do not like. It's important to learn your unique levels of emotions based on situations and circumstances. If you acknowledge and know that things are not right in a given situation, then seek help from someone that you trust first. Ask them to seek help too for themselves because this may be the first time that they have encountered this type of situation. Your emotional well-being is important. If you control your thoughts to think good during stressful events and situations, you will begin to lower your risk of emotional injuries.

Guilt & Anger

Sadness and loneliness harbor strong feelings that nobody can explain. Imagine a tear running down the side of a person's face when they are sleeping. This could only be a small example of the pain, hurt, and sorrow they may be feeling. Know that the feelings of guilt and anger may be lurking in every event they experience daily. To hide the pain, they may walk around half fulfilled and unmotivated. A part of the person is lost and can't get over what has happened.

Falling to the knees, praying, and pleading for forgiveness, help, and guidance occurs. It is only through the giving of yourself and feeling the true wants of others, as well as understanding your individual wants, will there be a cure for the ongoing pain that a person may feel. For example, imagine a person doing something that they feel has completely ruined their career or life. This can be physically, mentally, spiritually, or emotionally injuring someone else, themself, or both. It could also be something the person did that may be considered minor that damages a personal relationship. All of their life, they've known only one thing: the sport that they love. The thoughts that race through their mind determines their actions. If their thoughts are filled with guilt and anger, then negative outcomes will ruin their life. If a plea for forgiveness is done and is asked by the person to God, then and only then will they be set free, and the person can be judged.

Mental Change

After an injury, many thoughts run through the mind. When you recover, the thoughts are still there. These thoughts range from something small, such as getting more wrap to cover up a womb, to something big, such as asking and thinking to yourself, why should I go on? The negative thoughts and mental changes that a person goes through during and after an injury are detrimental to their recovery and future mental state.

Initially, the person will think and try to believe that they are the same person they were before the injury occurred. Acceptance that something major has happened must be made, and a plan must be developed to protect and secure future goals and aspirations.

The mind runs through many thoughts during this key time. Most will seem to be negative. Most individuals will give up and resort to drugs, alcohol, and other harmful habits. It is at this point that the person truly needs to understand what has happened to them. They also must begin to ask what needs to be done to protect their future goals and aspirations. This needs to be analyzed and examined to get over what has happened to the injured person.

Discipline & Passion

Never has what was done that was good in the past counted more. You've learned what a work ethic is all about. The passion that the individual possesses can push them to either unimaginable success or failure. There is no in-between with this. For example, if a person was disciplined as an athlete in most of their ways, then the process for recovery from an injury will be a challenge, but they have prepared themselves all along to overcome their current injury. If the person was not a disciplined person on or off the field or court, then the challenge is now to make a change in their approach to rehabbing their injury and how they prepare for success. Whether a disciplined person or not, a vision and passion for life beyond a particular sport must be developed, explored, and established. You exist for, as well as beyond the sport that you love. Leaving the sport physically and competitively, as you are and know, it will initially damage your emotional and mental state of mind. If you are able to bounce back and find yourself through personal development & discovery, you become limitless in the success that you can attain inside and outside of the sport that you love and cherish.

Rehab for an Injury

The power that's inside of you for a comeback is unlimited. Most individuals don't realize that preparation, discipline, and the ability to execute is developed and nurtured during this time of rehabilitation. Regardless of the injury, a person must commit to improving himself or herself. The thoughts of wanting to improve yourself are a message from God telling the person that "it's now time to build yourself for what else I have planned."

The elders and experienced will never be able to fully address an injury or rehab experience that has happened to you. They may have felt and experienced something completely different when it happened to them. You are unique. Listen to the advice that you are given but blaze your own trail. What I mean by this is that a person can have every resource available to them and will choose to either use it or not. Their way of life allows them to ponder on getting better by following a disciplined plan or not doing anything. On the other hand, a person who has no choice and doesn't have any resources must fully commit to a decision based on their belief or goal. This belief or goal will eventually decide their long-term fate in the sport that they love. If they are committed and believe strongly in improving themselves, then rehabbing an injury will be followed closely, and other areas of their true self will be discovered. Picture a person that is hopeless and understands what has happened to them. All they loved was doing one thing and one thing only. The ability to rehab fully and with discipline will allow this person to use all of the power that is hidden inside of them. They will become more complete as an individual if and only if they discipline themselves during this process.

Chapter 1: Injuries

Develop Your Game

Listen to the world tell you how they feel. Then use it as motivation to create greatness. The opportunity is presented to you at the moment when doubt from others cloud the earth. Only you and you alone can choose how to use the feedback you receive after an injury. Based on your choice, the development of how you play after an injury occurs. Whether you are from the ghetto, the suburbs, or another country, the word "Please" and "Thank You" will be constant. How you use and learn to use these words is key to your growth as an individual. In your own times of doubt and failure, say "Please" and "Thank You" to God. Ask for strength, courage, discipline, love, belief, and faith to get through your current situation. Say thank you too. Yes, this does matter and makes a difference. When you are working out and developing your game after an injury, going through workouts that you normally did before the injury occurred may be a challenge. This is something that will make you think negatively. Gain faith and develop a vision for your success in overcoming the injury and improving your life.

Give Back

Spirits of souls cry day after day. Answers are always given for individual actions, but the time a person must wait depends on their acceptance of God. Wishing, wanting, and fantasizing for worldly things disqualifies a person from the praying and asking that they are doing. Your loving heart must be pure and willing to give love to others first. How can a person truly know him or herself? The answer is to immerse yourself completely in a stranger's situation. Understand their why. Then give and help them unconditionally. This exact moment has actualized for you to make a change in your life. Give first. It will come back. Don't look for it; just let it happen. Let the universe work for you. God loves you, but you must give love as a person that was created in God's image. Believe this and live by it.

A Comeback

When none believes in you, true faith in God must be given. Understand that you were put in this situation to create or do something greater than your existence. Build character and devotion throughout your journey. Don't be afraid of failure. Take it in and discover the true you. Set and write down your goals. Nobody in this world knows what you are capable of doing but God. Trust in God. Pray and meditate daily in order to bring forth your gift to the world. You will view this as a comeback, but what's happening is that you are truly discovering the diamond that was hidden within you. The people around you will not give you support on everything that you do. Use this as added motivation to prove them wrong as well as to train smarter. You will come back from your injury or setback stronger, smarter, and better. The journey back will be worth it.

Chapter 2

Praying

<u>Art</u>

Laying awake at night calling for help is often felt through your soul. It hurts. No one is there or seems to care. What's next? This is a question that you are thinking about. Go back to the basic art of praying. You already know the entire prayer from beginning to end. The art of praying requires learning how to pray, which is something similar to finding your hidden gift. That is, you must learn what your prayer means for it to be effective in what you want accomplished. The pain that is felt and the discovery of the art of praying will alter the souls of those who discover it. Jesus Christ, The Holy Spirit, God, and the Kingdom of God are real. The existence of prayer will completely take you away from the physical world and set you at the altar of truth. There are strict and precise rules that you must understand in order to discover the Kingdom of God. It involves the giving of everything. Don't expect an immediate answer. It doesn't work that way. It's up to you to discover what you can do while you are on earth. This will test your faith and give you a true measure of the effects of your prayers.

Your heart will not be broken, but it will be restored to peace if you find what you can offer and give back to the world. This will open the door for you to do something that is greater than your existence right now. Don't sit and wait for an answer. You must be proactive in prayer. This requires you to view the entire process of praying as a beautiful painting that's worthy of waiting for answer to be set free. You must draw the painting first in your mind in order for you to be set free.

Chapter 2: Praying

Nothing Bothers You

It's hard to get to the state of being when an issue, event, or people continuously control your thoughts and bothers you. In the state of being, you are not mad, sad, happy, anxious, jealous, or envy. You are at peace. Understand that prayer during this stage is effective. You must be able to ignore the physical world and believe in the spiritual life at the end of the road. The peace that you feel opens your thoughts and mental state of communication with God. There is no substitute for being at peace with yourself and what's happening to you as well as in the world. The world is full of corrupt people, so expect oppositions to your attempt to being at peace. Test yourself by praying in peace daily. If what you produce is not what you want, then evaluate what you are doing and make the changes if they are necessary.

Belief

A true belief in the Holy Spirit, Jesus, God, and the Kingdom of God is needed to overcome situations and events that you may be going through. It's time to really analyze what you want out of life and what is true. Take time for prayer and meditation. Do it with a clear focus. An hour away from the material world will feel like you left a true love stranded far away when you finish praying. It's going to take everything that you got to give hope to a better tomorrow. When you take time for prayer and meditation with a clear focus, you walk away from worldly temptations and the physical world and begin to find truth, meaning, and your gift. You will also learn how to use your gift if you ask.

It's not as easy as I have just painted it to be. There must be direct communication with yourself and God. Develop complete faith in something greater than you and all that is seen in the physical world. An understanding that your purpose makes the world more complete based on every decision that you make will help you uncover truth. Know that you were born with a gift and that gift fits a piece of the world's puzzle. You must believe that you were blessed with the gift, pray for guidance, and believe that you can deliver your gift.

Heart

To hear God's voice, your mind (heart) must give love just as God does. Pure in the greatest form, the love from your mind gives the world and the people that you meet hope. When you pray, feel the love that God Gives. Be able to give pure love in thought, emotion, and what you are currently going through. The heart is the gateway to God's kingdom. Every individual born from a woman is born in the image of God, so you must love as God does. This means everyone that you encounter on a daily basis carries a piece of God within them. Look past their flaws. See the piece of God in them and love them for being. Their gift may be hidden or shining bright. The love that you give makes your prayers strong because God is love, and you must love purely from the heart to reach God.

How can a heart that's been crying and broken give love? you may ask. Well, remember that you made it through what you were going through, and it was because of your belief, love, and determination to what is true. That means that you know that love is important. God is love. What you went through was something that others may have made a different decision about. You went to the right person and took the right action. You were born to give love exactly the way that you give it.

Feelings of Loneliness and lack will be experienced on occasions. The feelings, thoughts, and emotions you have are temptations that bring you closer to divine truth. It hurts when the heart can't get what it wants. Continue to give love that's pure. This will create a path to serenity within your heart.

Practice

Practice has been a part of your life for many years now. It doesn't matter the sport that you participate in; you still practice to become the best that you can be in that sport. When you begin to pray, it requires the same approach and mindset when practicing for a sport. Yes, there will be failures, and just like the failures you experience when practicing a sport, you get back up and compete. Do the same thing when you pray. Compete. You may ask "What am I competing for?". You are competing for God's oneness. When you pray, practice every day to become one with God. No matter how many times you fail. Try again.

Examples of failures during prayer can be actions such as:
- Not paying attention when praying
- Quick prayers
- Asking for things that are not important
- Crying, Shouting, and Pleading
- Not praying at all

God already knows everything, so when you pray, you are really developing yourself to become more like God in order to help others in the world. Learn to become a top performer when praying. You'll find that oneness with God will open doors that didn't exist before. Don't just be a practice player when praying. Become elite. Pray and become one with God. Share the gift that is found within with others. Commit to giving all of you without judgment. Pray that your giving is enough to please God. What matters is the breath and love that you give to another person.

Open to Change

Throughout life, changes will occur in the world and in yourself. You have to realize that life is more than what you have been taught up to this point. It hurts to find out that all of your truest beliefs and truths were really false. To find out the true meaning of faith, follow what is whispered to you in the still of the night. Uncover the hidden messages that are given to you and change. Life is about giving all of you. A change in your core beliefs and ways must happen for you to give your all. Deep in your heart, you will find a willing gift of love that is waiting and wanting to be shared. The bridge that a person must cross represents how far the path to true love is. It requires everything from you. Love is pure. God is pure. Truth is pure. To discover true change, a person must love as God, and pure love must reign. Imagine an infatuation that you have for your favorite sport. You may think about it over and over again. Nothing compares to the deep passion and love that you feel about anything involved in the sport. Can you change your feelings about this sport? You will probably say no. Change is hard in this case. What if there was a passion, love, and pure truth that's greater than this? Finding this type of change, deep passion, and love will require you to go against worldly happenings without having a straight forward answer to your current problems. God works in this exact way. God requires you to be just because God is just. God is all everything. If you come from God and God is in you, then you must change the ways that you think. Start believing and loving as God.

Love

There is a journey that each individual must take in order to understand and accept love. A life that is filled with triumphs, emotions, and hurt is challenged by the wrath of love. Great kings, queens, and people have fallen because of love. Love is defined as an infinite passion for something.

Chapter 2: Praying

When praying, you must understand that God is complete and exact love. There is no higher love for something than the love that is given to you from God. When you pray, asking to give love as God gives love, enables and strengthens you to give as well as learn who you are. It hurts when time passes by and the hurt that you feel is damaging you.

If you have a dream for more, then you must interpret your life as it currently is and transform it to love others as God loves you. Beat the odds by becoming true with yourself. Remember that praying is an art. The love that you feel before, during, and after prayer is felt more if true love, belief, and faith are found in you by God. You've already asked for many things. They will be given. The true test is what will you give back with true love.

It hurts when someone you care about passes suddenly. It also hurts if someone that you care about is living, and they seem to live a reckless life. Coping with this trauma takes giving unconditional love. There never was a time in their life that a person who is about to die needs you more than now. Look past all of the events and pressure that you feel. In order to help and truly deliver that person to God will require love in every action that you put forth. Complaining, shouting, crying, and asking why me may seem not to be heard by God. Look inside of yourself and find out what you truly have to do to make the one that you love safe, comfortable, and content. Also, learn to understand how prayer affects love and love effects prayer.

Hope for Good

The life that you currently experience will pass. It will take time and faith to understand what your mind, love, and faith can do for you. Know that you not knowing what to do at this point is normal. You have to truly seek and find God. You must miss God's presence.

You must love God with all that you've got. Then and only then will you begin to feel his presence and not be alone.

The world is filled with deceptive traps that can capture your mind and actions. This sometimes leads to what seems like the purest hearts astray. Loving, believing, and giving your all, regardless of what is presented to you in the here and now, will unleash the true glory within you. All of the hope for glamour, fame, and money can't withstand the lonely heart that yearns for an answer to what life is about and what role your heart plays in God's plan for giving love to the world. Maybe this seems strange to you. Maybe this makes you question yourself and who you are—knowing that because you are awake to see another day here on earth gives you a chance to make history. You must hope for good and love in the world. When things and people show their bad side, this is your chance to become who you were born to be. The true belief in God that you currently hold will carry you through all pain and defeat that you experience along your journey. You'll find that your hope for good will define who you are during each stage of your life. Always love again and believe in what's good for the world. This will ultimately bring you closer to your gift and purpose for being.

Chapter 3

Giving Your Best

Alone

Imagine that you won't be here tomorrow. The feelings of being alone should fade. Being alone is a short-term gift if you use the time alone correctly. Find out more about the source that created everything. Find meaning. Find you. Listen. Pay attention to the world and its happenings. Life gives you many hints on what to do. It's up to you to uncover the clues. Most of the time, people seem to be full of guilt and sorrow about a situation or event that has happened to them. If, for one moment, the person stops and tries to thank God for just being, then maybe, just maybe the situation or event would open an opportunity to become a better person.

Being alone hurts if you go at it alone. That is, not doing anything at all except sulking in sorrow and blame. If this is done, loss over and over again occurs. Take being alone as the ultimate hint from God. This time was planned before you came into existence. It was planned for you to become closer to God. Ask God what you are supposed to do. Don't sob or plead. Just ask. Then sit and listen. It may take a day or even forty days. Regardless of the time, believe in the answer. In order to give your best when you are feeling alone and lost, you must meditate, listen silently, and become closer to God.

Coaching a sport at all levels has the responsibility to teach. Yet, athletes may seem to continue to struggle. It's hard to coach someone when you don't understand their life or what's happened to them. It's hard to coach someone when deep down the athlete does not believe in who they are. Normally, how to make it to the professional league is the main focus. This is similar to a lost ship being on sail to reach the next island that is seen. How can power be given to an individual if life isn't blown into them? True consciousness will help to understand this. To give your best, a complete breakdown and openness of starting over must occur. There will be many false teachers. Regarding the true individuals who really supposed to be in your life, you will go back to them and give thanks for something other than sport or money.

There is this fear that when you are alone, you may go crazy. This is false. Being alone can happen because of many reasons. The thoughts and feelings you have during this time are happening for a greater purpose than you. The state of mind that you are in, it may present feelings of hurt for being alone. Everything you are revolves around something or someone. Don't hold back your guilt about what you should have done. Forget the past. Being alone for the time period that you are in is a blessing and a destined moment in time. You have a choice during this time to either sulk in blame, guilt, and sorrow. The other choice is that you can discover true love and learn why you are here living through the feelings of being alone.

Being alone can be a time of missing out on all of the world's happenings, be it good or bad. Worldly happenings tend to focus more on failures, deaths, money, or wins. The truth about being alone is to discover how much you can continuously give with love.

Many times, there will be feelings of failures, loatheness, and sorrow because you are alone. You are made to find out how you can have it all. It starts by being alone. In order for you to give your absolute best in anything that you attempt, being alone opens up a vision for you to understand the deep down hurt that you feel and then go past that to see who you can be if you give your absolute best in any given situation. It's a choice that you have to make. A passion, a care, a love for getting out of where you currently are, drives the heart within you to seek salvation and clarity. Giving your best even when you are alone, it has a self-nurturing benefit that nothing or nobody in the world can provide. It's a stepping stone on your path to success. Understand that you were destined to read this book at this particular time. You will find your own truth within yourself by being alone during this time. I pray that you give your best.

Why It's Happening

You may have yelled out at the top of your voice by now, "Why?" "Why is this happening to me?" The feeling of the world crushing your hopes and dreams may seem to dominate your emotions. Many times, there have been clues that were given. This was done to prepare you for what was about to come next. The attention and focus needed to truly understand what's happening may be blurred by worldly distractions.

Up to this point in a person's life, the way the world works is understood and followed to a certain degree. What you will find is that there are many hidden answers that you must seek and find for yourself. You will become agitated and more focused on what you need to do to correct what's missing in your life and the world. To give your best when the most outrageous things are happening in your life, you must, in your mind, sort through and find or create a vision of success and happiness. The vision of success and happiness that you pose will work as a guide to answer all of your questions and strengthen your belief.

To give your best in sports, life, work, or in a relationship requires you to ask questions and then go on a journey to find out the answers to them. You become a seeker of truth. You'll uncover the answers to why what has happened or will happen to you happened. Seek with openness and true faith. What I mean by this is when you ask yourself, "Why am I doing this?" take a moment to truly understand what has led you to this point of asking this question. Be truthful to yourself by understanding and accepting the answer to the question that you've posed.

Knowing that it hurts to love alone will nurture your ambition. Love is brutal. It will swallow you whole and move on. I need you to love yourself like this. Know that what has happened to you has not happened before. You are unique in the eyes of God. You have something that you must go through wholly in order to give real love like God.

Tear After Tear

No one will seem to really understand you because of the mission that you were born to fulfill. Giving your best will hurt. You will cry over and over. Why? The people who are causing you pain and the world don't really understand what you have hidden inside of you. They don't know who you are going to be. They only see you in the present. The tears that are shed by you will help to build the future you. The heart, soul, and determination that you feel for that which you are going after will eventually be evident. To clearly answer the questions of "Why?" a person must pay attention to the gifts and blessings that are put into our lives. Understand that they are a hidden gift from God. These gifts and blessings are things that happen to you, people you meet, and the things you do to help others. You learn and grow a great deal during this time because of your past and present experiences. On and on, you must go to deliver the promise.

It may hurt to truly understand your gift and what you were born to do. Why? Because you are faced with a choice. That choice is to fulfill what you have inside of you or go astray. Most individuals face this moment of truth with withdrawal and depart from what is true.

They fold because of self-doubt. The destruction of the self leads to sorrow and tears. To overcome this, you must nurture your gift with the love from others. You must give love unconditionally too. Listen, read, and watch for messages from the footprints that were put in place before and during your time on earth.

Miracles are created upon each tear you cry. During this time, the pain of regret for not doing what you thought you should have done will overtake you. You will believe that there is no way out. You must give in and ask God to bless your tears and hurt. Heartbreak after heartbreak yearns for you to make a change for the better. Don't become blind from the views of others of a situation. Understand your pain and the tears that you've shed. Run to your dream. Live it in each tear that you've shed. Take the time to realize that it's OK to be scared. Face it. Take on the challenges of life and try not to let a tear run away without fulfilling and sharing your gift exactly how you see it in the world.

Incomplete

The heart yearns to be free. It seems as if your heart is just floating into the hands of God. Living, laughing, and loving makes the growth and journey of the person worthwhile. Failure, loss, doubt, and regret are God's test for you to love and give love as though none of the problems, worries, hurts, or guilt ever existed. One becomes lost in a state of being incomplete when worldly challenges affect the heart. Emotions take over and drown the person in self-pity and feelings of being incomplete. It takes trust and growth in the self to seek what is true. The only thing that is true in the world is the word of God. You have to find it because many false individuals have tried to change and hide the true message that was meant for you. This plays a part in why you are feeling incomplete. There will never be a greater love than what God has for his children and the world.

Chapter 3: Giving Your Best

A person has to do what God does in order to stop feeling incomplete. This first involves seeking and finding truth. Not what's been authorized by a dominant power. Fall in love with finding the true word. As you find information, more and more, you will know the truth of who you are and the answers to your deepest questions and wishes. Leave the world better than when you were born. Give unconditionally, sea to sea. Don't leave God.

Though you may have seemed to make it by the world's view, there will be a piece inside of you that is missing something. Day after day, your mind, heart, soul, and body will yearn for an answer to this riddle. The thought of being fulfilled has been a lifetime dream. You have finally got there, as so it seems. You may think that unanswered prayers may be a part of the cause of all the pain that you still may feel. This is false. You belong exactly where you are right now. It hurts because you feel and think that all is well too. However, you know deep down that it's not, and it hurts.

During this time of feeling incomplete, learn to find peace and serenity. Whether you are successful or have failed at something, don't give up. Follow the river. The river is a blessing from God. The river tells you to follow what's going good for you. Forget about everything that causes you pain. Follow the flow of good that's in your life.

Feeling incomplete is met with mixed feelings during times of despair. Agreeing with what's quick and easy normally is the solution. Earth, souls, and mankind depend on your life decisions. Though you are feeling incomplete, there is a way to become complete. Run to the river of good that's happening in your life.

Reality

Money or love are choices that will stream you to the truth. The things you do along the journey brings forth hurt. Hurt happens deep and strong, regardless of the path that's chosen. Know that where your state of mind is and how you choose to proceed determines the amount of love that's given to the world by you. It takes a clear understanding and evaluation of what the world is giving you. Compare that to the inner love that's presently within you. Detaching from reality and the worldly possessions, gains, and attributes will help you understand God. It may be different from what's preached by those covered with false realities. To be the greatest that you can be, you must seek forgiveness first. The vision you gain will guide you to the greatest reality of your life.

Having control of your own mind is the true riches of the world. Deceptive battles will be constant. To win this battle, you must eliminate anything that's mentioned of your inside thoughts that are not right by God. Thoughts of how the current situation may be good for you and make you happy may put you at a crossroads on what to do. Look at your face in the mirror. Speak for yourself and say, "God give the answer." You have to mean it. The reality of the situation that you are currently in will appear. Knowing what to do next will come to you, but it will take all of your courage to continue to seek and take action.

Keep Faith

If you give your absolute best in everything that you do and especially in your chosen gift, there will be many stones that will be turned over. There should be an ongoing belief in that which you can truly become. It will ultimately bring you to everlasting glory within yourself. Imagine for a second the places that you have been. Think about the failures that you have had. Continue to believe. It's a must in order for you to break through and give to the world.

After your pain of failure has subdued, a vengeance for becoming the best in what you can do is enlightened within you. Tears are shed because your belief never wavered. Save yourself, your gift, and the world by listening to God's whispers. The whispers will guide you to being free.

No person, circumstance, or failure will keep you from uncovering the truth. The hurt and regret will sometimes overshadow the true you. The hurt and regret are a lie. You must prove this by bringing your burning desires within you to life. There are no do-overs. The decision that you make during your times of despair must have true faith in what you believe. Then and only then will the truth be shown.

A New Beginning

Sealed with a kiss. This is how you should view your past. Each day, you have the ability to create a new and abundant world for yourself. Let God's rules guide you to the glory that you seek. Never forget what happened to you. Use its results as a lesson that you paid for fully through and through, regardless of the outcome. You have grown as a person because of what you've experienced. Nobody on this earth can exactly explain what you have lived through but you. You are you. Nobody can be you to feel your emotions. They can't think what you thought during the times of each of the events that you may continuously reflect on. What they can do is give their love wholeheartedly. It's up to you to open yourself (emotions, heart, and soul) to receive the love that's given to you. What most people do is use all of their heart, emotions, and soul to reflect on negative things that they have experienced in the past. It will take a deep understanding of yourself to discard these negative thoughts. Your heart will yearn for freedom. Let all that is negative go. Start today anew. Forgive, love, smile, and give your all. Lack of money, material things, and attention will never be needed to give true love that's from within. If you are able to see the positive in another person's most negative moment, a growth of love will begin deep inside of you.

Chapter 4

Family Values

Faith in God First

Imagine going a day without water. Better yet, try not to use water in anything that you consume or produce for one day. This is somewhat similar to the importance of your need to put God first. Make God your foundation, heart, soul, and the beauty of everything that you strive to do. Keep faith even when things or situations don't go the way that you planned them. Remember, success and happiness must be uncovered through your failures. It takes a lot to bypass all of the failures. During the bad times, faith in God and your true purpose for being born exactly how you are must be had. It is through your heart and faith that the love of God will be shared with the world. Your family values will nurture your faith. Be it good or bad, to understand your family values completely, you must know, respect, and learn from every lineage in your family. Yes, that means both of your dad's parents' linage and both of your mother's. Putting God first will help you to uncover truths. These truths must be accepted and used as a foundation to help you decide how you plan on giving unconditional love to the world.

Over and over again, thoughts will race in your mind about why a family member chose to do what they did. Let these thoughts go and focus on how it has shaped you. If you don't like the way that you've been shaped by it, then it's up to you to find God and give love to the world first. Then and only then will you begin to truly understand your thoughts about that family member or situation. It will be up to you to create new family values that shine bright throughout the world, even after you are gone from the earthly realm.

Find Out Your Lineage

There is no way around, through, up, or under it. To clearly find all the answers to the questions that you have about your family, you need to find out and learn exactly who the individual was that came before you. This entails reaching out to family members that you probably don't know right now. Uncovering the truth about who your father, mother, grandfather, grandmother, etc. were, puts you on a path to success. You may ask yourself, how will I be successful? First of all, the questions that you have about the person will diminish—no more relying on what someone said about them. You will gain clarity. Now, the challenge will be to interpret, accept, and learn from the truth about your lineage. Don't blame anyone for anything. Give love instead. Pray over and over again to learn and give love more. Finding your family lineage unlocks another door to success for you. You will always get a push back and stories about the person you seek to learn more about. Don't stop your search with the opinions of others that may know just as much about the person you are seeking as you already do. Exhaust all search choices during this time. The information that you gain about them must be valid. For example, you can find out if your family was enlisted in the military or not. The answer that you find is a valid one. Run to the truth. It will make giving more love to the world worthwhile.

Understand, Learn, and Respect the Past

Holding on to negative feelings because of what someone else did to hurt you or your family puts added trauma and anguish on you. The person that has caused you pain by not being in your life, not seeming to care about you, or abusing you has also gone through something during their early upbringing that has caused them to act and say the things they did. The amount of pain that people try to hold inside eventually causes them to do the opposite of what they may have set out meaning to do.

What the person did to you may have been wrong, or it may have been right; it's now up to you to use the negative energy, thoughts, and feelings that you have for the person or event to create a positive change for you and your family. How is this done? Well, just think about how much anger, hate, hurt, and revengeful feelings that you have for the person or event. By speaking aloud that you choose to give love and forgive when something has hurt you, it releases all of the negative energy, thoughts, and feelings that's inside of you. Sending that energy out into the world with love and forgiveness will send love and forgiveness back to you. Over time, you will master this strategy. It's not going to just happen quickly. It takes repetition. It takes having faith and being meaningful in your actions and the process of giving love and forgiveness.

Really try to understand, learn from, and respect the past. What has happened to you has now brought you to this unique opportunity to mold a new family that chooses to give unconditional love, forgiveness, learn from mistakes, and understand family members.

Envision your family members all happy and together at an event. What is everyone doing? What's being cooked? Who's dancing? What are the children playing? Who's sitting around the dinner table smiling and enjoying a conversation with you?

The answers to these questions will help you envision happiness, love, and forgiveness. Use the future vision that you have for your family to build up the motivation to speak aloud love and forgiveness. You will gain faith and meaning for why you choose to give love and forgiveness.

Raise the Standards

You were chosen to make the world a better place. In order to do that, an understanding of what you can do well must be discovered. A genuine love for a certain occupation, sport, or hobby already exists within you. Now, you must dig deep to become the best that you can be in that particular area. Natural talents and gifts already exist inside of you too. The time you spend getting better in your chosen area is similar to shaping a piece of wood into a finished product such as a table, chair, or house.

Raising the standards for your family values is done in the same way that you would strive to become your absolute best. This involves doing the right thing and making smart choices for your family's sake as well as yours. Generations after you should be able to understand and respect the new foundational standards that were put in place, practiced, and upheld by you for your family.

Examples of the new standards that I'm talking about are values and attributes such as being prompt, honest, loving, respectful, kind, giving, and knowledgeable. It doesn't cost anything to begin to implement these values and attributes into your daily life. Yes, it will be difficult to act this way towards all family members and people in the world. These same values and beliefs will return to you as you give them. As they may see the molding and growing pains you have gone through during the process, initially, everyone in your family may not accept the standards that you begin to put in place. Over time, the unaccepting individuals must learn to mold themselves by self-actualization and gaining an understanding of who they want to be.

Nurture Traditions

If there is something that is done to bring all of your family members together, then nurture it. Make it better. Make it grow. You may be saying to yourself that every time my family gets together, all they do is argue. Well, yes, this happens. It is needed to help shape and mold the entire family to withstand hurtful influences. The bond between family members may seem to strengthen more after something bad happens. Most families only see each other when a funeral occurs. Some families may argue and hold grudges after the funeral. This is all needed. The grudging family members, most of the time, have other issues going on in their lives, and the pain and suffering that they have from those issues may seem too strong to bear at that moment. Personal growth, love, respect, and understanding are needed by all involved in holding a grudge or being resentful.

More time must be taken to accept, understand, and love every family member. That doesn't mean that you must do what others in your family do on a daily basis. It doesn't mean to copy their philosophy about life. You will find that each family member is at a different stage when it comes to sharing love with the world. Each family member may have a different view of the family values that should be upheld. For example, a family member may always seem to say something at family gatherings such as "my dad and Granddad did it, so it runs in my family." In this situation, if what the dad and granddad did was nurturing for the family and helped the world in a good way, then the family member is saying it for confirmation and encouragement. On the other hand, if what they did was not nurturing for the family and caused more pain and suffering for the world, then the family member is saying it as a reason for confirmation for their own past and future failures.

If there is nothing that you can do to nurture a family tradition, begin a new one. Start slowly and carefully. When I say carefully, I mean, initially, don't try to organize a huge event and invite every family member that you know. Instead, create a plan. Take travel into consideration. Take work and personal matters into consideration too. After this is done, create a strategy to build a family tradition that grows.

Be the Connector

A smile is contagious. Others in the world are attracted to happiness. Yes, they are attracted to negativity too. However, being able to smile and bring forth happiness to the world requires an individual to elevate themselves to a new challenge in their life. This elevation occurs after the individual fails at something, and everything that could go wrong did go wrong. This elevation after a failure includes 1) A desire to overcome a past failure 2) An understanding of the knowledge, skills, and attributes that were gained from a past failure 3) Faith in success for the new challenge in your life 4) A winning smile even after a failure 5) A willingness to bring and share happiness to the world despite a personal struggle or failure.

By doing this, you become a connector to happiness and joy in the world. It brings out God's love that's inside of you. For example, a friend or family member that hangs around you may hang around you only because you make them feel happy. They use the time being around you as a positive self-pickup experience, as an escape from the negativity that's in the world.

Being a connector is not easy. It takes all of the strength and willpower that's inside of you to not only get back up after a failure. It also requires the individual to know what they are going to do next and have the confidence while executing what they have to do after they get up. They don't complain or explain. They smile and bring forth happiness to every other person in the world to help continue their own growth.

Respect Everyone

Answers to some of the most pressing issues in life can be found in the person, event, book, or task that you may be neglecting. Individuals may come and go in your life. Regardless of their age, sex, race, faith, or way of life, hidden within that person is a message for your life. Some of the people you meet may know their gift, and you see it and learn from it instantly. On the other hand, an individual that you meet may not be aware of their gift. If you are able to respect them by showing love, kindness, and understanding, it will help bring their gift to the surface. The closer the unaware person gets to their gift, the closer you will get to the message for your own. You learn and grow from their gift.

The outside appearance of individuals is similar to a fruit. Some fruit's outside texture may be soft—others, hard. They also come in different colors. Regardless of the fruit, there is a seed within it that makes it grow in order to share its gift with the world. Each person in the world can benefit from another by giving more respect to those they encounter. You'll be able to recognize if the person you meet is going in a positive direction or not. Respect them, despite whether they are a positive or negative influence. If they are a negative influence, use their shortcomings and mistakes to learn from them, and you don't have to continuously be around them because you won't grow. You'll only continuously grow as a person when you learn to accept everyone and continuously strive to improve yourself in all aspects of your life.

Give Back on Behalf of Your Family

Over the course of your childhood, certain family values were taught by your parents, guardians, or the adults in your life. These family values may have been good or bad. The good ones may uphold family traditions, contribute to worthy causes in the world, or enhance individual success. These family values will nurture future generations, and the individuals that practice them will continuously create opportunities to give back to society.

The bad family values that you witness may hurt you and have you always feeling bad. You may wish and pray that things were different. These values can be negative people, places, or things that purposely hurt the people in society or create negativity in the world. The burning desire that you have to change the bad family values can be used to create new family values. To do this, you should create a vision in your mind of how you want your family to be. What I mean by this is, if you could choose good family values that bring out happiness and the best in each of your family members, what would those values be? Once you have the family values described, picture in your mind your family doing those things. Then, you must begin to do those things, and by you doing so, it makes the people that you are around to eventually do the same things back to you.

For example, if your family seems to always complain at the service provided by the waiter or waitress when dining out, and because of this, they never leave a tip. This might be done on purpose, even if the service was good. To change this, begin by envisioning a happy and fun dining experience with your family. Then the next time you are dining with them, instead of waiting to hear a complaint, take the initiative to give the waiter or waitress a positive compliment. Smile and also take the lead to leave a tip for him or her. It doesn't matter the amount. If you can't do that, leave a pleasant note about how good the service was. This will cause you to create good family values and experiences that you want. It will also help you give back to the world on behalf of your family in a positive and nurturing way.

Chapter 4: Family Values

Change the World for the Better

You were meant to read this section of the book at this exact moment. There may be a lot of things that are changing in the world right now. The fear, anxiety, and feelings of hopelessness are broadcasted daily. God has put inside of you something special. That special thing is also a piece of God. It's an extension of the love that God has for all of the children in the world. You know exactly what to do to help others. Refuel yourself by spending time in the morning with God. The first hour when you wake up each day, lay in bed, and listen to God. Don't do the talking. Let whatever enters into your mind enter. Look past any and all things that are negative that enter your mind. You will know what message is given to you by God if it is helping all the people in the world. It's good for mankind. It changes the world for the better. You are special. You have been blessed with a superpower. Use it to give the love from God to the world.

As the world is changing, new gifts to the world are needed to keep love shared with all people in the world. The time and difficulties that you are currently experiencing will pass. It's like a scene from a movie. You can decide what the next scene will be because you are creating the script. It's important to listen to God. God will hold your hand as you imagine, write, and create the next scene. Your true happiness is ahead of you. Give love to the world to create happiness and love for others. Make it better.

Chapter 5

Advice From Others

Being Open

Nobody in this world knows or has the answer to every problem or issue. What they do have is the knowledge to seek out what they are looking for. It takes a level of humbleness from within to begin seeking. To unlock the future that you continuously dream of, you must learn from other people's experiences. Use their choices, advice, ways of thinking, and outlook on life to create a unique path of your own.

The thoughts that you may have right now may be similar to the following, "Nobody understands what I've been through. They can't tell me nothing that don't I already know." You are completely correct. What the person can do is listen and understand you. They can tell you about their thoughts, choices, and experiences in similar situations. Everyone that you encounter may not be able to relate to your exact situation. Your encounter with that individual has happened for a reason. It's up to you to be like a child and continue to seek. Your willingness to seek and learn from others will prepare you to use your own experiences to help others along your journey in life. Think of the advice that you get and learn from seeking as a clue from God that will help you uncover and deliver to the world what you were born to do.

Understand Their Perspective

One of the secrets to being able to seek is learning to put aside your own learned and deep-rooted views and perspectives about the way the world works. Then, when you are listening to someone else who has listened to your story, you should put your entire thought process and views of the way they see things at the forefront when they are giving any type of advice to you. This gives you the power to examine a particular situation from an understanding that may differ from yours about the situation. If you are able to let this happen, the magic of "giving" to the world starts to work. Let me explain. Over the course of an individual's lifetime, they have witnessed situations and listened to the advice given by many people from different backgrounds and walks of life. This individual then interprets these views. The interpretation of all of the collection of views that they receive depends on how much they set their own views aside and really try to listen and understand the other person. If a person is open to putting aside their own views, then they are able to collect the millions of perspectives from others that are inside of the person that they choose to listen to. They can now use the understanding gained to compare and contrast with other individuals that they choose to receive advice from. As this comparing and contrasting takes place, the values of each person that is talking to you may begin to take over and become expressed openly and visible. Other people have given them help or advice out of love as God gives love because the person that gave them advice cared about the person. Now, the person that is talking to you is sharing their own perspective of the situation. What they share with you is a gift, given out of love. As you may already know, some gifts may be bad, and some, good. You can use every gift that you receive to create and give a better gift to someone else. Taking time to understand another person's perspective will help open yourself up to becoming a giver of love.

Unique Life Experiences

This world will have many roads and hurdles to pass through. Knowing exactly who you are and accepting your own faults as learning experiences will transform you. It takes absolute faith in yourself. Know that you came from rock bottom to become the hero that you are. You did it. Your journey and what you've learned is unmatched. Nobody can repeat exactly what you did with the same strength, emotions, and effort you gave. They don't or can't understand your thought process during the moments of despair and doubt. The life experiences that you've successfully gone through has prepared you for this moment. It's now your turn to be a hero for someone in the world.

Just think about how many people are alive in this world. Think about how many people have now passed but took the time to write, speak, teach, or share advice about their journey. You were born to do great things. You must use all of your willpower to learn from other people's unique life experiences and also share your own. The ultimate truth will expose who you were meant to be. It won't just show who you currently are because you continue to seek, learn, and give.

Keeping Faith

If you are reading this now, it means that you are committed. You have faith in yourself. You have faith in the future. Most of all, God and you are walking together, hand in hand. I know that you've probably prayed over and over without seeing a quick result to an issue that's bothering you. It takes more than prayer to get results. You must face your own faults and accept them. Understand who you were, who you are, and who you want to become. Let go of the past. Everything that you will become depends on your absolute faith in what you choose to put into your future. Love someone else as you would love yourself. Really do it. Be the first one in something that helps the world. It will give you a small win and increase your confidence and faith. Arguments within your own self will constantly occur. What is happening is that the old memories and past events are trying to make the decision on what's to come in the future. Sometimes, it works. Sometimes, it doesn't. What is consistent in all of what's happened in the past is faith in God. God is the one and only one that can steer you toward the path that delivers what you really want out of life. Faith is pure. Faith is real. Discover what you want out of life and build faith. Ask for guidance daily. Do your own part in the world by giving the good that's within you. The good that is within you and the good that you do for the world will be an extension of the hand of God that walks with you and carries you during the difficult times.

Analyzing Other People's Success & Failures

Greatness leaves clues. Failure also leaves clues. The person that has experienced success or failure becomes equipped to help map out the future for others that are seeking God. The outcome of the situation or event that has been experienced matters in the fact of how it has helped others. A person can learn from bad experiences and get motivated to do better for themselves and the world. What a person chooses to take from the experience is what also matters. Burn and discard all negativity from bad experiences. Instead, go in and find something good that has happened because of the experience. It's like mining for gold. You have to discipline yourself to focus on the good in what's bad.

When analyzing other people's successes and failures, understanding their attitude, level of focus, and emotional state before, during, and after the experience helps you improve your own outlook of the world. The analysis has to be done without bias, prejudices, hate, or purposefully ignoring the truth of what has happened to the person and other people because of the event.

When you learn from others, it helps you design your own path in life. How do you learn from others? Reading biographies of others who were successful, listening to the stories of people in your life and those you seek out, and by putting yourself in unique situations to be around other great people. Again, you can learn from negative events and situations that other people have been through. Analyze how the person overcame the negativity to become successful. Ask questions and seek out the answers.

Choose to analyze the people who became successful because several things will always be constant. 1) They did not give up or quit 2) They walked with God, were carried by God, or became one with God 3) They had the determination to overcome the situation 4) They did it. They were successful.

Your Vision

The vision of the future that you have in your mind is proof that God loves you. That vision was given only to you to manifest it. All of your thoughts and dreams about this lasting vision acts as clues for what to do and what not to do in order to bring the vision that you have to life. A daily action plan must be developed and nurtured to form good habits in order to fulfill your vision. It also must be done and reexamined after setbacks in your life.

Advice from other individuals greatly stimulates your own vision because their vision for the future and your vision for what's to come combines and strengthens your desire. It provides momentum that must be acted upon by doing the small daily tasks to bring your vision to life.

The vision that you have for the future can include 1) a vision for yourself & family well-being 2) a vision for the world 3) a vision for a project, business, or way of life.

Talking about your vision with others will help you decide who you should spend your time with. Some of the individuals that you share your vision with will give you negative feedback. Others will motivate you instantly. Use both the positive and negative feedback that you receive to motivate yourself and provide fuel for completing daily tasks that must be done for you to manifest your vision.

Putting it Into Action

When a person that you know really loves you, and they give you any type of advice from their heart, you must listen to it. Give it the utmost consideration. The person who has given you the advice you are seeking is giving it for one of two reasons. They may be protecting you and don't want you to get hurt, or they had a very similar experience and have seen a better future for you. Careful consideration and reflection must be given to that person, the situation, and the advice given. Ultimately, you will become who you were meant to be based on the decisions that you make daily on your journey. Take your time to really dissect the advice given from those that truly have your best interest in mind and love you with all of their might.

In order to put what you truly want to put into action, you must walk away from your current beliefs and understanding of what is true. Use the advice that has been given to you with love and seek the answer to what you are looking for. The action that you take will ultimately decide the fate of your decision. Take action but understand the love that has been given to you. This love will guide you to a brighter path, regardless if you take the advice or not. It will make you analyze all areas of your life before you take action. A secret that I can share with you is the following: God has prepared the person that has given you advice with hurt, love, success, despair, and unanswered questions. They still have chosen to give. Use their giving hand to strengthen the world.

Giving Thanks

The journey that you experience will be unique and golden. It's filled with jewels of love to give to the world. Whether you had a bad experience or a good experience, the heart was nurtured, blessed, and built to give more because of the experience. Give thanks to God for being able to live and grow through it all. Give thanks to God for being able to provide a river of knowledge, love, and hope to someone else. Only you witnessed that particular event or situation here on earth in your physical body. Nobody else felt or thought how you did at that particular moment. God walked with you and carried you along each step of the journey.

By giving thanks, it prepares you for what is to come next. It gives you a guiding light and purpose. Each morning and night take time to send a message of gratitude to the almighty God. It makes your purpose and goals on earth even clearer to understand. You may become stagnant and resistant on occasions. Bounce back from each setback with a prayer asking for guidance. Always run to the truth. It will guide you through all of the storms of the world. You made it through your situation. Now, always remember to give thanks.

God put individuals with similar experiences, views, understandings, and beliefs within your reach. By listening, viewing, or reading others' advice, it should be analyzed, mentioned in prayer, and considered for its truth and underlying gift to the world.

Chapter 6

Read, Read, Read

Messages from the Past

Listening to the peaceful voices of the past is a must. Reading books of past journeys that are like that which you are currently pursuing or planning to begin helps you become better equipped with ultimate guidance and strategic know-how. It takes a level of humbleness to listen, analyze, and interpret what you've read in order to smile in the end. What has been paved and recorded before you decided to take on your current goal must be read over and over to make what is already in existence better for tomorrow's generation. Learn from the individuals' thought process as well as their intentions for making the world better. Reading a book is a challenge for you to do what is uncommon, and at one point in time, may have been unattainable. You have a nurtured gift that has been passed on to you. That gift is the ability to read. The true person that is inside of you will be shown to the world as you uncover, interpret, and visualize what's to come. Your heart needs to be pure and open to change. What you currently know may have been passed on mostly verbally. Use all messages, whether they are verbal, written, as well as what you currently see, to create the future. It's up to you to make a change for a better future. Read as many books as you can. Decide what to read based on where you want to be in 5, 10, 20, 30, and 40 years from now. It matters what you read. If what you are reading damages God's plan, then it's not worth reading. Find your passion and ultimate goal. Read books about others who have attempted the goal that you are striving for. The books that you read will open your eyes.

What's to Come

Based on a dream, the future can be made or destroyed. This fantasy moment of what can become real puts you in control of your destiny. Filled with emotions of love, the world grows because of what's in your heart. You must believe that God's purpose for you is true. Trust in the thoughts of goodness that come into your mind. It's a whisper from God.

Your emotions give strength to the thoughts you have. Control your emotions and steer them to what is good and just. Use good hunches, thoughts, your dreams, what's real, and the positive whispers from the voice inside of you to bring forth good to the world. Break through and learn from what happened in the past. Regardless of your current position in life, you were born to lead. The leader that you were meant to be is only uncovered if you are willing to take the hand of God, believe, and listen to the good whispers that come to you. Actions on what's been given to you must be taken to truly give the world what's to come. Believe.

Becoming who you were meant to be

Time alone pondering where you came from should be done in seclusion. Take a journey away from the world and all its strife. Analyze what's truly important in the world, then pray for an answer to the questions you have. Temptations of fame and money should be regulated and completely eliminated from your true mission. You become ready to receive who you were meant to be once you put aside worldly possessions in exchange for giving worldly gifts.

Be willing to read, study, analyze, and filter the gifts that were provided by others in the world. Your love for a thing will make what you were meant to be an obvious choice. Listen to your heart. Eliminate distractions by searching for the original source of your ultimate goal for happiness if you have feelings of despair, guilt, and hurt. Use the deep love that you have for that one thing to guide you to what's true. You will overcome many things in life. Becoming who you were meant to be may require you to do what's uncommon. Trust in your passion and belief in what is true. It will guide you to what was promised. Ultimately, your oneness with God will deliver what was promised without measure.

Being Free

Your heart has been broken, you've lost everything, and you've suffered deep pain. The tears are overflowing, and the world seems cruel. Don't walk out on yourself. This has happened for you to become free from all pain, hurt, regret, and everything bad that's in the world. It liberates you from the past. It's up to you to learn and go on. You become free to use what has happened to you to create love and happiness. Crying alone night after night sparks a flame for desire. You become free to use your passion and desire to either bring more hurt and pain to the world or mend the tears and hearts of God's children. Time limits your freedom, so understand that you only become free for a particular time in which the power, love, and spirit of God fills you and provides liberation to others who seek to become free. You control the time that you want to be free.

Persistence

When all hope, motivation, and love seem to be gone, there is a hidden power within you that propels you to not only get up, but it will give you more strength to give an even greater effort than what you've already given. The level of focus and commitment is without measure. The determination to obtain your dream takes the ability to channel all the love that you have towards your ultimate goal. You must wake up and understand that the current failures or doubts that you are experiencing happened many times ago. Come back and believe in what you were meant to do.

Persistence delivers all of your dreams to the world. The level of determination that you are able to build paints the picture for a future that is true. Remember all of the hurt, defeats, ridicule, and letdowns that happened in the past. Use them as logs to a fire for an everlasting burning desire to achieve. The strength needed to keep a sound mind after being defeated is found by seeking only God. Seek what is true in everything that you pursue. Every journey will have people, things, events, and resources that can both help you or hurt you. The preparation that you choose to do beforehand will guide your decision. This is why reading is of the utmost importance. I believe in you. Feel it and make it happen.

Uncovering Living Habits

Your guiding light (goals) for your future should ultimately determine your daily habits. All of the worldly temptations are continuously attacking your senses. These temptations control whether you read daily or not. They also control what you choose to read. It takes awareness, persistence, and a clear focus to take back control of your own senses. By doing this, you gain control of your daily habits. Failures will occur. What you go through in order to gain control of your daily habits is similar to training or practicing for a game, match, or other sports event. When you are training, it takes your ability to do drills and workouts in repetitions. Uncovering living habits that you currently have requires you to take a clear and honest evaluation of what you are doing with your time within a typical day. Examine how much time you are wasting doing things that are caused by worldly temptations and distract you from your goals in life. Once this is uncovered, find out what time of the day that you feel:

a) The happiest
b) Most clear-minded

c) Full of energy, confidence, and motivation

d) Free in thought and emotion

Choose these times during the day to complete the most important goals in your life. Have integrity with yourself to read, develop, and take action on your life goals. Plan out your entire day, hour by hour. After planning your day, take action, and do the tasks that you plan. This helps you to develop and gain control and power over worldly temptations. Your will power, determination, persistence, and understanding of what is true is also needed.

Uncovering the Truth

By reading something that nurtures your mind and well-being daily, it will help you to uncover the truth about the things that you are seeking along your journey in life. Train yourself to develop the skill of reading. Each truth that you find out will lead you to an understanding of what's to come. It also prepares you to take action on what you were meant to do in life.

Everything that you read needs to be dissected and analyzed for authenticity, as well as for the help it can give to all of God's children. Each day, there will be worldly distractions that will attempt to grab the attention of your mind and time. A careful plan of action to eliminate or control these distractions should be made on a daily, weekly, monthly, and annual basis.

To uncover truths about what you are seeking, it's going to require you to do things and tasks that contribute positively to your overall health, well-being, and mental state of mind. The wisdom and understanding that you will gain unlocks unexpected doors of opportunity. It will be up to you to decide to act on each opportunity and give love to the world.

Chapter 7

Learn and Make History

<u>Invest in Yourself</u>

As the sun continuously shines its rays of light on the world, it serves as inspiration and faith in how successful you can become. You must keep getting up and rise above all negativity daily. Investing in yourself is the ultimate challenge. When I say challenge, I'm talking about, for example, everything else that may be going on in your life may be put first and at the top of your list of things to accomplish. People sometimes put doing things for themselves last. It's Ok to do this, but you must still continuously invest in yourself.

There are several ways to invest in yourself. They are:

1. Continuously learning
2. Exercising
3. Finding oneness with God
4. Enhancing your professional skills
5. Giving love and time to what you believe in
6. Making yourself smile
7. Setting goals

Continuously learning involves reading books that inspire, motivate, and share knowledge, taking classes, attending self -improvement seminars, and talking with individuals that have reached goals that you are striving for. Exercising involves you creating and taking action on a daily plan to do some form of physical activity that will improve your health and longevity. Finding oneness with God takes you on a mental and spiritual journey that will provide truth and serenity. Enhancing your professional skills involves improving and using the skills that you have effectively. An example of a skill set would be public speaking. If you are good at public speaking, try to use the skill daily as well as earn income from it if possible. On the other hand, if you have a skill set that you are weak at, let's say it's interpersonal skills. Begin learning and practicing how to make your interpersonal skills as good as your public speaking skills. Giving love and time to what you believe in will help you develop a sense of purpose. It touches your heart and strengthens your belief that you can make a difference in the world. Making yourself smile involves doing, saying, and experiencing things and events daily that will make you laugh and smile. This relieves stress and gives you an uplifted spirit. With low stress and an uplifted spirit, you will be able to complete more of your daily tasks and goals.

Finally, setting goals involves creating a destination for who and where you want to be in the future. It helps you decide what you will be doing in the future and how you will do it. Your plan to get there includes daily, weekly, monthly, and annual tasks that must be accomplished to get you to your ultimate goal.

Investing in yourself is a way to build a new you for the present and the future. As you invest in the various areas that were mentioned, your level of giving back to the world should increase. By giving more of yourself to the world, new opportunities will continue to be presented to you.

Using Your Gift

All of the power you have to make an impact on the world is found in your natural gift that you were blessed with at birth. Despite the countless hours you've committed to developing a skill in a particular sport or endeavor, your natural gift can be found by you searching within yourself. Sometimes you really know what you can do naturally. You know what action you feel you should do to help the world. A gut feeling or message whispers to you, suggesting an action for you to take. Within that gut feeling and whisper is found your gift.

In order to use your gift daily, learn how to harness self-discipline, self-love, and the ability to take action. The world won't demand you to do this. The glamour of fame, deceptive media that's viewed by most individuals, and the trap of doing what's deemed as ordinary daily tasks most of the time gets in the way of a person being able to share their natural gifts with the world. Become aware of what you do daily. Remove worldly temptations. Then take time to look inside of yourself. Do this peacefully and calmly. Close your eyes and imagine yourself helping a person, group, country, or the world. Paint a picture of how that person or group looks. Then listen to your gut and what is whispered to you about what you are doing to help this group. You naturally see a problem and how you can solve it. Take action to begin using your gift to make the world better.

Whether you believe in God or not, you still were blessed with a gift that's inside of you. Whether you believe in God or not, or do not currently believe in anything, take a moment, step back and ask yourself the following three questions:

1. Who was I born to be?
2. Why was I created?
3. How can I use my gift to help the world?

Then continuously seek the answer to these questions. It will lead you to what is true.

Understanding Why You Were Chosen

You were chosen to bring heaven to earth. You make the world happy by unconditionally releasing your gift. World events happen daily, which causes drama, guilt, and sorrow. At this moment in time, you are needed to let go of your gift and create a smile. You were chosen because of what's inside of you. This is something that you have to find and harness. The journey to do this will make and mold you into who you were meant to be.

Love should always be unconditional. Give it freely. It will return to you when you need it the most. A heart can choose to give hate or give love. Immerse yourself in what is true. Uncover the signs and clues to your hidden gift. When they see you again, your face will glow because you know the reason why you were chosen to help the world.

Imagine a world free of pain and sorrow. Imagine a world where there is no hate, jealousy, or deceit. Imagine if everyone had success within their own unique gift that was given at birth. Imagine a world where all signs of love point to what a person has created as a gift to the world. You were chosen because hidden deep within your thoughts and imagination is a world that is true.

Becoming Your Best

Year after year, you will strive to become better. Each tear that you shed because of what you did not do provides fuel for your future success. Only you can give the greatness that is within you. It takes you getting back up after a failure to truly reap the benefits of what's to come.

Search within yourself for what is true. God plants his mark where you can always find it. Given this fact, your unconditional trust in yourself will bring you closer to the light. To become your best, you have to embrace failure, ridicule, hurt, and loss. This sometimes has to be done with an inner smile, knowing that something great is still to come. Constantly or overly mourning over a loss or failure develops bad habits. Lift your thoughts and focus towards what you are planning to accomplish. Ignore anything that comes to your mind that is negative. Reject it.

Grow and nurture all of your thoughts, hunches, whispers that are true and good for the world. Becoming your best will drop you to your knees, but this is where you truly need to be at that particular moment. Take advantage of the time on your knees and pray that you can become closer to God. Anything in this world is possible. If you can put your prayers, mind, imagination, and beliefs behind you becoming your best; the best within you will shine bright throughout the world.

What's Been Done Before

Sometimes what's happened to you in the past may have left you with a negative view of the world. You must know that this experience and the feelings that you felt had to happen. It's similar to watering a plant so it can grow into something beautiful. As you go through the various stages and experiences of life, take time to analyze what's been done before within your family's inner circle. This will help you truly understand the people you love most. A person's happiness becomes fulfilled in the happiness of another person.

There will come a time in your life that you will need help with getting through personal and professional situations. In order to grow and prosper, seek the success results of individuals who have gone through what you are currently going through. Become like a child that yearns to learn something new. Be the child that falls, cries, but then gets back up and tries again. Time goes by fast, so specific planning, analyzing, and taking action must be done, regardless of the situation or result.

Heroes

Through all the rain and storms, the heroes that you looked up to will push you to the next level. Understand that the insight they gave you and put inside of you is true and meant to be. Your hero was born to make you great. To fully grasp what was given to you, analyze the hero's heart. Look at the struggles they overcame to give a gift to the world. This is leadership, love, and giving back to the fullest.

A hero is a person that chooses to sacrifice certain worldly temptations to bring forth God's will. The person has gone through a lot in their lifetime, and despite the struggles, cries, and failures, they chose to give love to the world. Unmatched by anyone that you will ever see on media vices, a hero sows their love daily in unexpected ways. These ways will always be remembered by those who are most connected to the message. Time has gone by, and the hero that you looked up to may now be gone. Your whole life as you know it has been altered because of this loss. What was left inside of you is a permanent blueprint of what is true. God's will is wrapped within the truth that's inside of you. Listen to your hero. Follow the path that was paved up to the point that you know a new path must be paved for the good of the world. Your hero believes in you. God believes in you.

Seeing What's Not There

A better world exists in the mind of those who don't give up on their dreams. A positive picture of what's to come fills the inner sight of a determined person. Never before has the picture in your mind been seen. Nobody nowhere can promise a better tomorrow the way you have chosen to create it.

To see what's not there takes faith in yourself. You must find yourself by not dwelling on past wrongs or failures. The yearning desire and determination that you feel propels the perfect picture in your mind of what can be. Can you imagine if you really understood what you could harness and create? The mind of a person is similar to the largest ocean in the world. The depth and clarity that you reach are up to you. Finding a reason to explore yourself will cause amazing things to happen. Give your all when you do this. As a result of learning more about yourself, what you see or imagine for the future will be molded to fulfill your growth.

Create a picture of love, happiness, success, and what's good by God. Your feelings must be steered to do what is good. Emotions of what negatively happened to you will try to blur your vision. It is at this moment that you must stand up to yourself. Do this over and over again until you are successful and what you envision in your mind is true and good for the world.

Positivity

Your heart needs to see good, think good, feel good, and do good daily. This creates a temporary world that nurtures your long-term growth. I say that it's temporary because your thoughts change every second that you live. The control you have over your thoughts makes who you will be daily. When you think of good things for yourself and the world, then good things will come to you.

Having a positive attitude and thought process can create magic. The unspoken word holds power. The spoken word is the most powerful. Once released, it searches the world for a person, group, or community to leave an impact on. If you decide that you are going to give your best daily, think, say, do, see, and envision all things that are good. The hardest part in doing this is dealing with the people and worldly temptations that you encounter daily, because they are mostly negative. By consuming negative things, it damages your inner core. It creates lasting pains and illnesses. You are special. You've come too far in your life not to make a change. Don't get discouraged if it's difficult to make a change. It may also be hard to think of positive things daily. It's a challenge that you will eventually master. It takes you being able to fail, get back up, and keep a positive attitude and thought process.

Chapter 8

Give Back

<u>God's Will</u>

In order to truly maximize the gift that you were blessed with at birth, you must put God's Will first in everything that you believe in or do. The soul of a man becomes filtered with untrue exterior thoughts of what's to come. Your willpower, determination, and faith are not enough when it comes to clearly designing the future of the world. God's Will reign supreme. This is why you must trust what's sent to your heart, as well as the deep love that you have for what is happening to you. When the time eventually comes to decide what to do, the clues have already been given to you all along. Use God's Will as your guide to make it happen.

I know it hurts to give love and not feel that anything is given back to you. This feeling is preparation and nurturing for your future blessings. God loves you unconditionally. Built inside of you is unlimited power, knowledge, and love to overcome, create, or change anything in this world.

<u>Your Passion</u>

What's burning inside of you was put there for a reason. Take God's hand and embrace your full desire, thoughts, and feelings for a specific purpose, cause, or event. The passion that you have for something is the underlying fire for what you can give to the world. You must believe in yourself, God, and the feelings that you have for what it is that you truly want to do. It hurts deeply to love something that doesn't love you back. This may be something that you will experience initially. That doesn't mean that what you feel, believe, and want to do is wrong. It means that you are uncovering the truth about your purpose to the world, and you are in the initial stages of finding out about who you really are, what you can do, and where you can go.

Passion unmasks the future quickly. The underlying journey to pursue and fulfill your passion is ultimately up to you to obtain. Mold yourself into a better person by making a change to do something different that you know deep down inside is good for the world.

Building self-esteem and discipline is a must. Passion for anything requires total commitment. You have this naturally. Understand that a passion and a gift crosses road only when action is taken daily.

Doing It For A Change

Over and over, you've seen how the world has played out. Even though changes are mentioned and upheld by some, the attempt to divorce what the world is currently delays the outcome. Don't cry for what you lost. You are special. Change can only happen through belief. The one who can protect their heart from the world are fortunate but not exempt from failure. Those that have hearts that have been tampered with truly decide what's to come next. Build your mind. Seek truth. Happiness is exposed when what's currently fuzzy to you becomes clear. Life on earth requires you to continuously seek the truth in order to make a lasting change. Hurt, struggle, pain, success, and triumph all play a part in the growth of what you create. Every mountain has a certain path that must be taken to get to the top. What's inside of you has been paved for you to get to the top of your gifted field. You belong there. This is what was given to you at birth. The only thing that's missing is you fully accepting your gift and giving thanks.

World Problems

To give the world a kiss, you must understand why you want to kiss it. There have been many things that have caused happiness and sorrow in the world that we currently know. Blind happiness makes what seems true good for all. The real truth leaves even the simple soul left to wonder and ask, "Why Me? Why This? Why Now?" To answer these questions wholeheartedly, a person needs to look at who's influencing their current path paved for the world. Find salvation in Jesus Christ and what is to come. Distraction after distraction will cause you to blame problems that have already been solved.

The world needs you to become who you were meant to be and live a life that solves problems. Prayers to God give you power unmatched by any title that can be given to you in this world. Listen to the voice within you and be a giver of what's true. In the end, judgment will be passed on everything. Be it misery or happiness, a solution exists to make the world better.

Parents Pride

Whether they are there physically or not, your success, failures, and perseverance were seen, acknowledged, and blessed with love by God and your earthly biological parents. You may have gone through a lot in your life up to this point. What waits ahead of you has been prepared for you by our father, God. Your parents nurtured God's will in order to create an opportunity for your perseverance, triumph, and success to become what is true.

There is a right and wrong way to give blessings. When notoriety and fame are guiding something that you plan to give to the world, then the wrong message and foundation will be established on earth. God gives love unconditionally. God forgives and creates what's to come through you. Being recognized for doing what is true will be acknowledged and found when those who seek it need it.

Uncover the truth within you. Understand your parents for who they are. Accept it. Find the hidden gift that they continue to nurture within you. As with Jesus Christ and your parents, you may not physically get to see every accomplishment that you helped prepare for the world, but you will leave what is true by God. Your parent's pride for what they did will be sustained, appreciated, and given with unconditional love and dignity to the next generation. It's up to you to make a future parent's pride that's positive.

Mourning A Loss

The pain is felt deep when you lose someone that you truly love. The time that was spent with the person seemed to be brief, inconsistent at times, yet unforgettable. Continue to pray to God and love that person. The heart of that person has been given to you. It's inside of you if you seek God, what's true and what that person was attempting to give to you.

Never before have you felt a pain that hurts so deep. Use the time that you spend in guilt, sorrow, and regret to begin a new path that is true by God and for what's to come. They hear your cries and prayers. The message back is "Make It happen" . God loves you. The person that you lost loves you. Being able to see them again would make your world complete. You would not need to do or think of anything else. The person that has passed knew this day would come. They stayed around on earth with God's blessings long enough to make sure that the gift hidden inside of you to the world was nurtured enough to have it blossom and shared with the world.

Molding The Future

The love that you choose to give to someone else helps to create the future. What's in your heart is pure, just, and true. The exact way you choose to share love to others may vary, but it will be the exact way that it was meant to be. You've been through a lot and may still be recovering. Certain people may appear in your life to help you develop yourself as well as create a future that is molded by the good that is inside of you because you chose to share it with that person.

Bring it out of you today. In order to give your all, you have to get the most out of yourself daily. If you are not around the people that you have chosen to mold, then you must prepare a way that the gift that's inside of you can be passed on. Believe in what's true. Believe in yourself and your vision for what's to come that's just and true. Give freely.

Give birth to what's inside of you and watch it fail, grow, and give to the world. That's what every mother has experienced. Mothers give gifts to the world. Everyone has something inside of them that they can give to the world better than anyone else. The pain that you experience while delivering your gift is similar to the labor pains that a mother has when giving birth. Once you see what you've created, naturally, a feeling of 'there's nothing that would stop you from seeing that gift grow and prosper as a valuable treasure to the world' exists. Nothing can stop you from creating and giving to the world but you. It hurts to the core going through the growth pains that you experience. Pay attention to who you run to when you are in despair, as well as who you blame for your failures during your journey. Most of the time, it's the mother that's there to help you carry your cross through the storm. Whether it's your mother, father, or another special person that is there for you, examine the type of unconditional love that they chose to give to you during your darkest moments and use that as an example of how you can mold the future to make it better for someone else.

In order to give freely, remember that you must see the good in every person that enters your life. This may seem very hard to do because your past experiences and advice received from others have molded your thoughts and views. Let the love of God shine through by seeing what's good in a person.

What you've experienced in your life up to this point is unmatched by others. A stare into the window to your heart for a lifeline brings forth solutions that are hidden within you. As you develop yourself, it may include giving to others during your current period of development. You may say to yourself, "I'm at one of my lowest points and can't speak to anyone right now." The signs to improve one's self are given to you and buried inside of you. These signs are touched and improved by the people that you encounter that need or even ask for your help. Give thanks to God for the opportunity to be a part of his kingdom. Then deliver what was asked of you without judgment or regret.

Flying alone is what the greatest birds often do. There is a miracle that builds inside of a person that needs undeniable belief. This must be done alone in the presence of God. God believes in you. Now, it takes an understanding of what you've experienced. It may hurt. It may make you the happiest ever. What your experience has built for you is a song that only you can sing in the right way to move another individual who is seeking forward. It doesn't matter what the seeker who looks to you has experienced. They will take what is given and fly in their own way, just as you did.

What's inside of you is true. This is where clarity, belief, love, and your gift meet in order to create what's to come. You are in control of what you release. There is no other way to witness heaven on earth than to unleash what's deep inside of you to the world. Being yourself is unique. The tears you've shed helped to build you into who you currently are. You may right now be undecided on whether to give love to the world that's true, accept the way things are, or give up and let what happens occur. Do you remember the love that was given by that one person that told you that you were special? They said it over and over again to you. You may have just ignored it at first because you didn't believe what they were saying. They may now be gone from this world. At that past moment in history, that person that told you that you were special, they were able to see inside of your heart and believe for you. It's now up to you to believe in yourself as well as give unconditional love and belief in others.

Exhale. The good that you give to the world will shine a light on the ones who are seeking it. They will naturally understand, relate, and know what to do. The good that is inside of you was released correctly in this case. To witness the release of the good in a person in a wrong way, look at worldly deceptions and temptations used on another.

You are special beyond measure. When you create good for the future of the earth, you give a special kiss from God when the person that is madly searching for what you are giving truthfully in the eyes of God receives it. Your heart will lead you towards the wind that blows in the direction of the truth. Pray as much as you can that your gift that you deliver is blessed and blown by the breath of Jesus Christ. The person that receives it will know precisely what to do next.

Gratitude

The changes that you have experienced over the years were done purposely. You are gifted. The changes in you had to happen in order for you to become better prepared to receive the gift that was given to you with love from God. God has prepared you, and only you to bring forth the gift. Protecting your gift is done naturally by God. No matter how hard someone tries to imitate what's inside of you, they can't do it in your own special and blessed way. To really understand this, just look at a set of identical twins that are born into this world. On the outside, everything seems like that they are the same. A closer look inside both of them shows that they are different. From their fingerprints to their every thought, the identical twins are given a unique gift that's sealed with a kiss from God. The only thing that's missing at their birth is a faith strong enough to seek the Kingdom of God. In order for their gift to be fully developed and delivered to the world, they must learn to seek what is true.

Time alone was meant to be within God's presence. You must seek God and give thanks for all that you've been given up to this point in your life, as well as everything that you are preparing to receive. Giving thanks for the things that are taken for granted on a daily basis liberates your spirit. Everything in the world may seem like it's going bad and that nothing can be done to change it. Sometimes, escaping and getting away from all of the worldly happenings and drama is what's needed for you.

There are moments in time that you will feel like ending it all and not going on. There also will be times that you hope and wish will never end. Each moment in time must be used as a learning experience to learn to give love to the world and give thanks to God for blessing you by getting through what you've experienced.

The love of Jesus Christ is stored deep inside of you. Imitate Jesus in every way. Gratitude begins with Jesus Christ. Jesus Christ was born with a gift and delivered it to the world. The belief, love, and faith in what he was doing were blessed by God along his entire journey because Jesus knew how to communicate with God, and he knew what the Kingdom of God held in store for man. The type of love Jesus gave to the world and to God was put inside of you for you to nurture and give freely to the world. You must seek God in order to truly give your gift.

The Kingdom of God will never be truly understood by a mortal person. It takes walking away from what is known and seeking what is unknown. The journey begins and ends with the unique questions that you have about what's going on within yourself and the world.

Chapter 8: Give Back

Seek what is true, and you'll begin to establish loyalty in God's Kingdom.

Be thankful for the unique gift that you were given by God at birth. Only you can do it. It's very different from a skill that can be developed. You nurture a gift by experiencing the world's ups and downs. You develop a skill through practice. Uncover what your gift is and take every experience in life as an opportunity to nurture your unique God-given gift. Give thanks for your unique gift. You know exactly what it is but may sometimes put it to the side because of worldly happenings.

Jesus did the most amazing things for others in the world. Follow Jesus Christ's lead and give more of yourself. Give more because you can. It's up to you to truly decide what to do with your life. You have the willpower that can strengthen or weaken your gift. Take time to walk away from everything that's currently going on in your life and think about just you and what is really true as it pertains to worldly happenings and the Kingdom of God.

Chapter 9

Getting What You Want

<u>Seek The Kingdom of God in Everything You Do</u>

Continuously study yourself inside and out for all that is good. Seek truth in everything that's outside of you. Then share what's good and true with the world.

In the name of the Father, Son, and Holy Spirit, may Jesus Christ bless you with wisdom, understanding, and love. I pray that you share all your blessings with the world and love as God does.

Bonus

In His Own Words

Some things happen for a reason.
Like the constant flow of greed through each season.
Life was made to forgive a soul's downfall.
But what is a world if it's not made for all?
As I ponder on life's greatest tasks,
I'm still left with questions that you ask.
You are all the same, whether race or creed.
There's still always one common flaw; greed.
Though this problem will continue to exist.
It should occur to you that a life's at risk.
You may be separated by regions and beliefs.
I'm still real to all and those who seek.
Unconditional love and harmony is the answer.
Those who believe will be the ones who prosper.
There may be pains throughout this dance.
A change without knowing gives you another chance.
Holding on to the future is the key to all prayers.
Although yours were answered, don't forget theirs.
These are my words, and I believe this to be true.
I know there's a chance. I believe in you.

By David Carl Smith Jr.
From the book *Answers to the Struggles of Life* by David Smith

A Birthday Wish

Visioning your happiest moment brings your smile to life.
It takes me away from the days' constant strife.
Anytime, anywhere, I dedicate the world to you.
My hearts filled with love and a dream that's true.
I remember your last words; hug, and kiss.
Just one more time is this birthday wish.

By David Carl Smith Jr.

A Basketball Wish

As the stars light up the sky on a hot summer night,
The sound that's heard causes some to take flight.
With unwavering force, it goes on and on.
Many stare, wondering when will it be done.
Walk after walk and street after street,
The challenge that's given is to not miss a beat.
As the night grows old, nobody's there.
There's a pause in the road, along with a prayer.
It started with this, so I pass it with a no-look dish.
This... Yes. This is my basketball wish.

By David Carl Smith Jr.

From the book: *Champion's Vision* by David Smith

www.ingramcontent.com/pod-product-compliance
Lightning Source LLC
Chambersburg PA
CBHW071004080526
44587CB00015B/2344